ECONOMIC JUSTICE
IN AN UNFAIR WORLD

ECONOMIC JUSTICE IN AN UNFAIR WORLD

TOWARD
A LEVEL PLAYING FIELD

Ethan B. Kapstein

PRINCETON UNIVERSITY PRESS

PRINCETON AND OXFORD

COPYRIGHT © 2006 BY PRINCETON UNIVERSITY PRESS
PUBLISHED BY PRINCETON UNIVERSITY PRESS,
41 WILLIAM STREET, PRINCETON, NEW JERSEY 08540
IN THE UNITED KINGDOM: PRINCETON UNIVERSITY PRESS,
3 MARKET PLACE, WOODSTOCK, OXFORDSHIRE OX20 1SY

LIBRARY OF CONGRESS CATALOGING-IN-PUBLICATION DATA
KAPSTEIN, ETHAN B.
ECONOMIC JUSTICE IN AN UNFAIR WORLD: TOWARD A LEVEL
PLAYING FIELD / ETHAN B. KAPSTEIN.
P. CM.
INCLUDES BIBLIOGRAPHICAL REFERENCES AND INDEX.

ISBN-13: 978-0-691-11772-0 (HARDCOVER : ALK. PAPER)
ISBN-10: 0-691-11772-1 (HARDCOVER : ALK. PAPER)

1. DISTRIBUTIVE JUSTICE. 2. INTERNATIONAL ECONOMIC
RELATIONS—MORAL AND ETHICAL ASPECTS. 3. ECONOMIC
DEVELOPMENT—AND ETHICAL ASPECTS. 4. ECONOMIC
POLICY—MORAL AND ETHICAL ASPECTS. 5. INTERNATIONAL
ECONOMIC INTEGRATION. I. TITLE.

HB523.K358 2006
337'.01—DC22   2005025182

BRITISH LIBRARY CATALOGING-IN-PUBLICATION
DATA IS AVAILABLE

THIS BOOK HAS BEEN COMPOSED IN JANSON

PRINTED ON ACID-FREE PAPER. ∞

PUP.PRINCETON.EDU

PRINTED IN THE UNITED STATES OF AMERICA

1 3 5 7 9 10 8 6 4 2

This book is dedicated to the memory of Raymond Vernon

CONTENTS

List of Tables   ix

Preface   xi

List of Abbreviations   xix

ONE
Economic Justice in an Unfair World   1

TWO
Fairness in Trade   45

THREE
Allocating Aid   86

FOUR
Justice in Migration and Labor   114

FIVE
Harnessing Investment   147

SIX
Toward a Level Playing Field: A Policy Agenda   175

Notes   197

Bibliography   219

Index   235

TABLES

1.1. Three Models of International Economic Justice   7

2.1. Concessions Received and Given during the Uruguay
Round (SMM)   62

2.2. Industrial-World Tariff Escalation   68

4.1. Immigration to the United States, 1991–1998   121

4.2. Types of Labor Standards   138

5.1. The U.N. Global Compact   170

6.1. Judging the Global Economy   186

PREFACE

Economics without ethics is a mutilated
science—the play of Hamlet without Hamlet.
—Washington Gladden

I f any norm characterizes international economic relations, it is probably that they should be carried out
on a "level playing field." But across a wide range
of issue areas, including trade, finance, investment, and
migration, the economic agents who are involved—including states, firms, labor unions, and individuals—often
complain that the global playing field is tilted against
them. How to level the field has therefore become a topic
of widespread debate, particularly in the context of an international system in which the distribution of wealth and
power is highly skewed.

Developing countries, for example, routinely argue
that agricultural protectionism by the United States and
the European Union denies them the opportunity of exercising their comparative advantage in cotton, sugar, and
other commodities, and thus the possibility of export-led
growth. Labor unions point out the inherent unfairness
of a global economy in which capital is freely mobile but
workers—particularly unskilled workers—are not. And
around the world, oppressed groups, often women and
ethnic minorities, find themselves trapped in poverty with
few avenues for escape either at home or abroad.

But what would a level playing field look like when it
comes to the world economy? One finds divergent views

on that question. Some would argue that a level playing field can be created only by redistributing the earth's scarce resources from those who are rich to those who are poor, implying that reducing welfare for the one will necessarily increase it for the other.[1] Others focus on the need to reform the major international financial institutions, whose bureaucracies and operations are often criticized for serving the status quo interests of wealthy and powerful states and their peak economic interest groups. These proposals reflect profound differences regarding the very definition of a level playing field and how to create one. Clarifying the issues at stake is crucial, for as Trollope's Mr. Melmotte said, "you should know what justice is before you demand it."[2]

The purpose of this book is to advance the debate over what constitutes a fairer, more just world economy—a level playing field for global economic transactions. Specifically, I elaborate a "liberal internationalist" perspective on the level playing field, meaning that my primary normative concern is with economic relations among states (as opposed to among firms or persons) and the well-being of each state within the international system. I assess global economic relations in terms of whether they are *inclusive*, *participatory*, and *welfare-enhancing*, and I describe arrangements that meet these three criteria as being of "mutual advantage." By inclusive I mean that the state has membership in any regime or organization that writes the rules for its international economic transactions, by participatory I mean that the state has a voice in writing these rules, and by welfare-enhancing I mean that the state benefits more from its inclusion and participation in the regime than it would from its exclusion.

To be sure, in good utilitarian fashion, a welfare-enhancing regime need not give a voice to every actor; it could simply produce "the greatest good for the greatest number." However, it is my contention that sovereign states will seek participation in arrangements that affect their well-being, will question the legitimacy of institutions that deny them a say, and will promote only those regimes that enhance their individual well-being. In contrast, it is difficult to imagine that governments would accept as legitimate international structures that influenced their fate without seeking their input. It is in this sense that my framework is a liberal or "individualist" one.

Admittedly, the scheme that I am proposing will strike some readers as woefully inadequate in that, given the fact of widespread poverty and destitution, and tremendous income gaps between rich and poor persons and countries, a case can be made that leveling the playing field requires a lot more than I offer here; it demands instead a significant reallocation of the world's wealth and resources. But I cast doubt on the political merits of proposals that depend on economically meaningful redistributions from country A to country B, for the simple reason that many governments would oppose such programs on the grounds that they are welfare-reducing from their individual perspectives. At the same time, I hope readers will come to appreciate that even the modest conceptualization that I am advancing has surprising power in illuminating the normative structure of international economic relations, and points the way toward politically feasible—because they are welfare-enhancing—reforms of the system.

To illustrate the value of a liberal internationalist perspective, let us consider the structure of the World Trade

Organization (WTO), which writes the rules for global commerce. Although the WTO is broadly inclusive, in that its membership is near universal and its agreements extend to every state based on the principle of "most-favored nation," it is not fully participatory, since its underlying bargaining structure is grounded in the norm of strict reciprocity. In practice, trade liberalization agreements are negotiated mainly on the basis of mercantilist, tit-for-tat reciprocity, meaning that if you open your market to one billion dollars of my exports, I will do the same for you. This structure favors liberalization among the great economic powers with their large domestic markets, particularly the United States and the European Union; after all, why should trade negotiators from Washington and Brussels waste their precious time and political capital negotiating with a small African economy whose markets are of little interest to their exporters anyway?

Trade liberalization based on strict or tit-for-tat reciprocity makes it difficult for the smaller developing countries to play in the trade sandbox, since they have little to offer industrial world negotiators in terms of market access that is of compelling interest. They therefore remain largely outside the trade negotiations, and as a consequence their interests—say, in global agricultural liberalization—are underrepresented. What results from this structure is a trade regime that is less welfare-enhancing for many states—for example, those with a comparative advantage in agriculture—than it would be were an alternative principle of participation in negotiations adopted, say, one in which the differing bargaining capabilities of nations was explicitly recognized. In fact, in most of the regimes that govern the global economy, developing countries have only limited influence.

But why should states, particularly rich and powerful states, even care about building a fairer global economy, a more level playing field? Why not just extract rents from developing countries, in colonial fashion? Building on insights from economics and game theory, as well as moral philosophy, the answer I develop for why fairness matters in international economic relations emphasizes self-interest. Our multilateral arrangements for trade, finance, and investment are more likely to prove robust if they are viewed as serving the economic interests of *all* their member states, generating outcomes that are accepted as fair through inclusive and participatory procedures that are widely considered to be legitimate. Conversely, unfairness will provide dissatisfied actors with incentives to alter the status quo, perhaps violently.

Readers will quickly see, however, that my interests in this book go beyond theoretical exposition. One of the great weaknesses in the application of moral philosophy to international politics is that it has almost exclusively been exploited by scholars as a normative tool for asserting what some imagined world *should* look like, as opposed to a methodology for helping us to understand the world as it *is*. To be sure, the task of the moral philosopher is primarily to produce arguments on behalf of desirable futures, no matter how difficult these may be to achieve in practice.[3] But the downside of such exposition is that it gives the literature a tone that is preachy rather than analytical. Such a normative approach has little appeal for scholars, officials, and activists, who are often trying to understand the causal forces behind international problems and the public policies that states formulate in response to them. The theory outlined here is thus written on the cusp of political philosophy, international relations, and economic theory, in the hope that, to use Richard Dworkin's phrase, it "responds to politics."[4]

The book has six chapters. The first chapter lays out my theory of international economic justice. The following four chapters provide applications of that theory to the cases of trade, aid, migration and labor, and investment. The concluding chapter offers reflections on contemporary public policy and thoughts for further research. As the reader will see, my focus in each chapter is on developing countries, and an issue that I continually raise is whether the existing economic order can be justified to them, and if not, what changes must be made in the name of greater fairness.

I am extremely grateful for the support that I have received from several institutions and many individuals during the writing of this book, notably INSEAD and my faculty colleagues there; the French Institute for International Relations (IFRI); the Center for Global Development; and the German Marshall Fund of the United States, which awarded me a Transatlantic Fellowship during academic years 2003–2006. Many of the ideas presented here were initially developed while I was on the faculty of the University of Minnesota, and I wish to express thanks to my colleagues and graduate students at that wonderful institution. I am particularly sorry that my former Minnesota colleague Robert Hudec did not live to see the publication of this book, given his pioneering research on developing countries in the international trading system.

Special thanks are owed to Nancy Birdsall of the Center for Global Development, Antonio Fatas of INSEAD,

Craig Kennedy of the German Marshall Fund of the United States, Branko Milanovic of the World Bank, Thierry de Montbrial of the Institut Français des Relations Internationales, and Joel Rosenthal of the Carnegie Council on Ethics and International Affairs, who have provided guidance and assistance throughout this project. Christian Barry, Charles Beitz, Dan Esty, Dimitri Landa, Lisa Martin, Thomas Pogge, Richard Steinberg, and Oran Young provided detailed comments on individual chapters, and helpful ideas have been offered by participants in seminars at Cornell, INSEAD, the National University of Singapore, Oxford, Sciences Po, the University of Washington, and the Wharton School, University of Pennsylvania. Chuck Myers at Princeton University Press supported the project at an early stage and has been more than generous with his guidance and advice throughout the long process of completing the manuscript; Princeton's anonymous outside reviewers also provided painstaking critiques of earlier drafts, and I wish to convey my gratitude to them. I owe Benedicte Callan special thanks for living with this book, taking its ideas seriously, and not kicking it out of the house!

I have dedicated this book to the memory of Professor Raymond Vernon, the great scholar of international economic relations and of the multinational enterprise. Many years ago, when I was a postdoctoral fellow at Harvard University, Samuel Huntington urged me to speak with Ray about a research project. That is the best career advice that I have ever received, and in short order Ray's influence went far beyond my life in the academy. Ray was a true mentor in all senses of the term, and I am grateful to have shared so much time with him.

In the process of writing this book, I have been forced to question some of my long-standing notions of international economic justice and in many instances have had to revise them. This is largely a result of my ongoing effort at matching normative theories with models and data to join the "ought" with the "is." If this work helps others to advance a progressive research and public policy agenda with respect to economic relations among nations, my hopes for it will have been largely fulfilled.

LIST OF ABBREVIATIONS

BITs	bilateral investment treaties
CLS	core labor standards
CPIA	country policy and institutional assessment
FDI	foreign direct investment
FPE	factor price equalization
GATT	General Agreement on Tariffs and Trade
GDP	gross domestic product
GSPs	generalized system of preferences
IFRI	French Institute for International Relations
ILO	International Labor Organization
IMF	International Monetary Fund
IOM	International Organization for Migration
LDCs	less developed countries
MDGs	Millennium Development Goals
MFN	most favored nation
MNE	multinational enterprise
NGO	nongovernmental organization
OECD	Organization for Economic Cooperation and Development
PRGF	Poverty Reduction Growth Facility
PSR	potential settlement region
S&D	special and differential
TAPLINE	Trans-Arabian Pipeline
TRIPS	trade-related intellectual property rights
UG	ultimatum game
UNCTAD	United Nations Conference on Trade and Development
WTO	World Trade Organization

ECONOMIC JUSTICE
IN AN UNFAIR WORLD

1

ECONOMIC JUSTICE
IN AN UNFAIR WORLD

*The place of morality in international politics is
the most obscure and difficult problem in the
whole range of international studies.*
—E. H. Carr

Recent years have witnessed a growing number of
activists, scholars, and even policy makers asserting that the global economy operates in a way
that is fundamentally unfair, particularly to developing
countries and to the poor within them. Thus, a Washing-
ton-based policy analyst has called the trade policies of
the United States and the European Union an "ethical
scandal,"[1] and a U.S. trade representative has branded European protection of its agriculture "immoral."[2] The Bel-
gian foreign minister has proclaimed the need for an "ethical globalization,"[3] and the former United Nations High
Commissioner for Human Rights, Mary Robinson, has
even launched an "Ethical Globalization Initiative." As
president of the World Bank, James Wolfensohn lamented
that "something is wrong" with the global economy, and
his controversial chief economist, the Nobel Prize–winner
Joseph Stiglitz, once glibly remarked, "Of course, no one
expected that the world market would be fair."[4]

In response to the global economy's alleged inequities,
we now find the United Nations regularly publishing re-

ports with titles such as *Globalization with a Human Face*, and debates over the international community's poverty-reducing "Millennium Development Goals" making front-page news.[5] But profound disagreements exist over how to solve the world's most pressing economic problems, and who should take responsibility for them.

Despite this lack of common ground, it is probably safe to say that almost everyone agrees that economic transactions should be carried out on a "level playing field." As a consequence, even the president of the United States, who governs the world's lone superpower, finds it necessary to offer assurances that his international trade objectives include "providing a level playing field for American workers."[6]

But what does it mean to create a level playing field for international economic transactions? And why is such leveling even desirable? After all, there are prominent theories of international relations that dismiss the notion that world politics can or should be conceptualized in normative terms at all. Most prominently, "realists" assert that there is no moral authority above states, no central enforcement agency, and so states are "self-contained" ethical units. This means that world politics is shaped by the distribution of power rather than by any shared normative culture, and thus a tilted playing field is quite "natural" and perhaps even desirable, to the extent that a great power uses its authority to create the international regimes that make global economic transactions possible.

Given differing views about what constitutes a level playing field and about the sources of unfairness in the global economy, this chapter opens by providing three alternative lenses for viewing the normative problems associated with increasing economic integration. As we will see, some people criticize increasing economic integration because of its allegedly deleterious effects on *national welfare* and the domestic social compact, or what might be called the *communitarian* model of economic justice. Others, in contrast, are primarily concerned with the effects of greater openness on the "global poor," or what might be called, following Derek Parfit, the *prioritarian* variant of *cosmopolitanism*; this means that international economic policy should make poverty reduction its priority.[7] Finally, still others, including myself, emphasize the political structure of the global economy, its international institutions and regimes, and how these institutions shape economic relations among nation-states. That is the particular focus of this book, and I label my perspective the *liberal internationalist* approach to economic justice; elaborating that framework is the major burden of this chapter.

Models of International Economic Justice

Even within the institutional setting provided by domestic politics, in which a central authority can (at least in principle) set taxes, redistribute incomes, and provide social safety nets, there are few public policies that are as controversial as those that shape the allocation and redistribution of assets, revenues, and other scarce resources, that is, the policies that constitute a society's definition of economic or distributive justice. (*Distributive justice* is more accurately a broader or "umbrella" term of art, referring not only to economic goods but to opportunities and other valued services—e.g., health care—as well, but I will also use it in this narrower context here.) Students and practitioners of economic or distributive justice are concerned with the goods and services that should be subject to allocation and distribution (e.g., income, health care), the recipient populations (e.g., "needy" individuals, particular ethnic or religious groups, or developing countries), the distributive principles (e.g., equality of resources or of opportunity), and the specific policy instruments (e.g., progressive taxation schemes or foreign aid transfers).

Naturally, there is significant debate among scholars, public officials, and citizens with respect to each of these dimensions, that is, *what* should be distributed, *who* the recipients should be, *what* distributive principles should be adopted, and *how* those allocations should be accomplished.[8] As Thomas Schelling has written, "Among the most divisive issues that policy deals with is the distribution of income and wealth," and of course he might have added other things as well, such as "opportunities."[9]

As already noted, common to every domestic theory of distributive justice is the assumption of a central authority, a government or a state, that is capable of enforcing initial allocation decisions and any subsequent distributions that a society may wish to make. Thus, Ronald Dworkin's theory of equality of resources "requires government to adopt laws and policies that insure that its citizens' fates are, so far as government can achieve this, insensitive to who they otherwise are."[10] Similarly, the realization of Hal Varian's theory of fairness depends on a state that distributes property "equally to new generations" and serves "as a watchdog to prevent monopolistic interference with the market."[11] Even the late libertarian philosopher Robert Nozick, who viewed the complete theory of distribution as the voluntary exchange of legitimately acquired property, recognized the need for a minimal "night watchman" state and admitted that an even stronger central government might be necessary to rectify historical injustices in transfer.[12]

Despite the fact that states have long been "globalized" in terms of their economic relations, it is only in recent years that scholars have begun to pursue the problem of distributive or economic justice on the wider stage provided by world politics.[13] We have already seen that this effort is marked by considerable controversy and is rejected outright by modern realist thought. Can "international justice" even be said to exist in the context of an anarchic system that lacks a central enforcement agency (recall Hobbes: "where there is no law, there can be no justice")? And if we assume it does exist, who are the relevant actors in this particular drama? Are they states or individuals? Resolving these issues is of considerable importance if we wish to advance theoretical, much less public policy, debate.

Stanley Hoffmann has asserted, with considerable reason, that "the problems of international distributive justice are by far the most troublesome" within the study of international relations.[14] Hoffmann's point is that even if we boldly assumed that states cared about establishing a system of international justice, it would hardly be a straightforward exercise to determine how they might go about distributing wealth (and power) in a way that promotes public goods such as global peace and prosperity. Some scholars have argued that justice among nations would require a more or less radical redistribution of the earth's scarce resources, such as oil and minerals; others, including myself, look askance on policies that would reduce welfare in a particular state, and instead emphasize the role of free trade and investment in promoting economic growth; these differing views are developed in this book. Further, disentangling domestic from international economic justice, especially in light of increasing globalization, poses a first-order challenge.

To date, scholarly (and indeed, activist) assertions about international economic justice—or injustice—have taken at least three distinct forms, which reflect contrasting views about the normative consequences of increasing economic openness. Table 1.1 provides a matrix that summarizes these frameworks, and the following sections provide brief descriptions of them.

The Communitarian Critique

First, some critics of today's international economic order are primarily concerned with the effects of globalization on *domestic* social and economic arrangements, or what I call the *communitarian* model of economic justice. This group takes domestic society as the appropriate site of distributive justice, for it is only within this political context that coercive fiscal and redistributive policies can be introduced (usually by the state), as a way of reducing income inequality, poverty, lack of opportunity, and other collective "bads" in a manner that is consistent with the domestic social compact, the "basic bargain" between state and society. In this view, global economic integration is tilting the playing field against the social compact, particularly in "cradle-to-grave" welfare states, which are allegedly threatened by capital mobility and a growing inability to meet collective objectives through redistributive taxation. Questions that are relevant to communitarians include: How has greater openness influenced poverty and the income distribution *within* countries, and particu-

TABLE 1.1

Three Models of International Economic Justice

Theory	Site	Policy goal
Communitarian	Nation-state	Equal opportunity
Liberal	Society of states	Growth and convergence
Cosmopolitan	Individuals	Poverty reduction

Source: Author

larly within "my" country? Has it closed income gaps or widened them? Who are the "winners" and "losers" from globalization (or market integration) within domestic societies, and can the losers be effectively compensated? What are the effects of greater openness on domestic fiscal and social policies and on the capacity of the state to maintain the domestic social compact among its citizens? These questions reflect a predominant concern with the effects of global economic pressures on domestic societies and with the capacity of the state to respond in a manner that preserves domestic distributive justice.

John Ruggie's "bargain of embedded liberalism"—the phrase he used to describe the postwar "Bretton Woods" order—provides perhaps the neatest expression of the national welfare or communitarian position.[15] According to Ruggie, the challenge for postwar leaders was to rebuild a global economy that would be made safe for the welfare states of Western Europe and North America. A dense network of domestic and international arrangements was crafted in order to ensure that global trade and investment did not undermine the goals of nationally based social policies, such as full employment and equal opportunity.

Thus, international trade agreements included "escape clauses" to protect workers, and particular industries were exempted altogether. Conversely, the United States and other countries put into place "trade adjustment assistance" and other compensatory mechanisms to support those who were hurt by economic change. In short, greater openness was to be made consistent with and to reinforce the domestic social compact. And for a while, many if not most had reason to remain confident in this model, at least in the advanced industrial countries. The expansion of global commerce following World War II was accompanied by the rise of the "cradle-to-grave" welfare state, particularly in Western Europe.

It is the fear that rapid globalization is disrupting this communitarian model of distributive justice that has sparked an intensive research agenda in recent years on the relationship between greater openness to trade and investment on the one hand and, for example, changes in domestic income distribution, employment, and poverty rates on the others.[16] As Dani Rodrik has written, "the international integration of markets for goods, services and capital is pressuring societies to alter their traditional practices, and in return broad segments of these societies are putting up a fight."[17] In an important review of the literature, William Cline has demonstrated that greater openness to trade has increased wage inequality in the United States, as unskilled workers face competitive pressures from imports made with low-wage labor. Reflecting the communitarian model, he writes that the "basic policy conclusion" stemming for his analysis "is that a commitment to open trade needs to go hand in hand with a commitment to a whole array of *domestic policies* that help ensure that society evolves in an equitable rather than an inequitable direction" (emphasis added). Tellingly, he nowhere suggests that *international* policies might need changing as well.[18]

Mainstream economic theory and public policy analysis reflect the communitarian perspective in important respects; after all, the state remains the privileged site of policymaking and the actor with the monopoly right to use coercive means over its own territory. Economists commonly hold that "countries shape their own destiny," and endogenous growth theory emphasizes the role of domestic institutions and policy choices in promoting investment and creating human capital. From this standpoint, globalization offers states tremendous opportunities to increase their technological base through trade and foreign direct investment, and in turn improves their chances for sustained growth. Yet one question that communitarians pose is whether the "rules-based" economic regimes that currently structure international economic relations are making it more difficult for states to pursue such growth-promoting domestic policies, say, through the use of "protectionist" instruments or subsidies, because these are now illegitimate. Further, globalization may undermine the state's fiscal capacity to redistribute income from winners to losers, and thus the social compact that binds citizens together.

In short, communitarians emphasize the effects of greater openness to trade and investment on the capacities of domestic societies to provide adequate economic opportunities for their members, and particularly for unskilled workers in industrial nations, whose incomes and livelihoods may be "threatened" by globalization (including by immigration of low-skilled workers) in a meaningful way.[19] To these groups, the potential benefits of globalization may be elusive, at least over a relevant time horizon, and particularly if the state is now unable to help them adjust through fiscal transfers and education and training opportunities. Communitarian critics, then, have raised significant issues of international economic justice, but through the particular lens of national welfare.

The Cosmopolitan Challenge

The second group of globalization critics we consider is composed of *cosmopolitans*, whose main concern is with the effects of greater openness on individuals, and particularly the poor, irrespective of national boundaries, since these frontiers have no particular ethical relevance. The World Bank economist Branko Milanovic has deftly described this perspective when he writes, mimicking Diogenes, "globalization implies that national borders are becoming less important, and that every individual may, in theory, be regarded simply as a denizen of the world."[20]

Cosmopolitanism provides, in fact, a big theoretical tent. But as one of its leading theorists, Thomas Pogge, writes, "Three elements are shared by all cosmopolitan positions. First, *individualism*: the ultimate units of concern are human beings, or persons. . . . Second, *universality*: the status of ultimate unit of concern attaches to every living being equally. . . . Third, *generality*: this special status has global force."[21]

Because it is such a big tent, I focus more narrowly in this book on those cosmopolitans who might be called "prioritarians," following Derek Parfit's term of art.[22] The specific question that prioritarian theory raises for modern globalization concerns the effects of economic integration on the poor and least advantaged, and prioritarians argue that public policies should give absolute priority to their plight. Pogge, for example, has recently asserted, "the affluent countries and their citizens . . . impose a global economic order under which millions avoidably die each year from poverty-related causes,"[23] and that this order should be reformed for that very reason. This global order and its associated rules influence poverty levels and income inequality within nations, by favoring particular interests (e.g., those of multinational firms) over others (e.g., labor). Indeed, it is notable that although the rules governing trade and investment are relatively strong, the rules governing labor rights—much less basic human rights—are weak.[24] These are stinging accusations of the international order, for which prioritarians demand a response.

Cosmopolitan thought holds that rational persons may agree on certain universal moral truths, and it is these truths that provide the normative glue, weak as it may be, that holds domestic societies, and eventually the international community, together. They thus perceive the promise of a "universal international society grounded in the gradual homogenization and globalization of norms. . . . This development has manifested itself in a variety of ways . . . most significantly, in the growing acknowledgment by states and societies that all individuals, regardless of their citizenship, race, religion, or other defining characteristics, are entitled to basic protections of life, property and contract."[25]

The cosmopolitan perspective is not only influential in contemporary political philosophy, but it has become increasingly influential in the world of public policy as well. The present-day preoccupation of the World Bank and International Monetary Fund with global "poverty reduction," for example, cannot be neatly explained by reference to the "objective" material interests of powerful states. Instead, this emphasis indicates how ideas—specifically new ideas concerning the site of distributive justice in light of economic globalization—have come to shape the priorities of the leading international institutions.[26] We will return to this theme in later chapters.

Many nongovernmental organizations have also appealed to cosmopolitan values in seeking public support for their activities. The British charitable organization Oxfam, for example, claims that its members are "global citizens" who seek "global equity." The organization presumes to speak for "poor people," placing their "rights and interests" at the center of international power, identified as being wielded by global corporations, multilateral institutions, and national governments. Similarly, Save the Children lobbies "for changes that will benefit *all* children, including future generations" (emphasis added).[27]

In making their normative assertions, prioritarians often evoke a utilitarian perspective, suggesting that global happiness would be maximized by distributing income and wealth away from those who enjoy relatively little utility from the marginal dollar or euro to those who would gain high utility from receiving additional sums. Thus, the marginal dollar of income is probably of less value to Bill Gates than to a smallholding coffee grower in the Chiapas region of Mexico. What this implies is that economic justice is found internationally, as it often is domestically, through redistribution schemes. As Milanovic asks, "If the political community becomes the world, would it not make sense to define redistribution at the world scale?"[28] Similarly, Pogge has proposed a "Global Resource Tax," the proceeds of which "are to be used toward the emancipation of the present and future global poor."[29] Even Britain's chancellor of the exchequer, Gordon Brown, has proposed an "International Financial Facility" to increase spending on foreign aid targeted at the poor, and President Jacques Chirac of France routinely floats the idea of a "Tobin Tax" on international financial transactions in order to finance development. Whatever the practical merits of these proposals, they indicate the cosmopolitan sensibility of treating people, qua ethical "units," as members of one universal community, each of whom has a claim on the world's resources.

It must be emphasized that cosmopolitans take seriously, in a way that many other theoretical traditions do not, the problems of state failure and of unjust states. While recognizing that states *could* serve the cosmopolitan end of a social arrangement in which each individual is treated equally or fairly, they also accept that many governments around the world lack the will or capability to provide for the basic needs of their citizens, especially those citizens who, owing to income, gender, religion, or ethnic background, are most vulnerable to life's vicissitudes. Cosmopolitans simply reject the notion that the bad luck of certain persons to find themselves locked up in states that deny basic human needs, much less basic human rights, is reason enough for those of us who are more fortunate to turn our backs on their plight. As a consequence, "cosmopolitans have argued that efforts to secure justice should focus on the reform of social arrangements beyond the nation state." In this book, we will consider some of the proposals along these lines: for example, the oft-heard calls for tying international trade agreements to "higher" labor standards.[30]

The prioritarian view of international economic justice poses a profound set of theoretical and policy challenges. While not denying the roles and responsibilities of national elites in extracting rents from their societies and oppressing the poor, this position forces us to ask whether the international arrangements that shape the global economy—which were, of course, designed by these very same elites—actually help or hinder the life chances of the world's most vulnerable citizens, no matter where they live, or whether they simply serve as vehicles for the rich and powerful. If the entire story of international institutions can be reduced to the interests of the privileged few, then one must be pessimistic about any chances for reform—at least peaceful reform—since these institutions' architects, who represent the dominant interest groups, are unlikely to have much motivation to share their part of the pie with others.

Although I am sympathetic to the prioritarian model of international economic justice, and appreciate its decision rule—that social arrangements must promote the life chances of those who are most vulnerable—it is not a framework that I emphasize in this book, building instead what I consider to be a largely complementary, statist approach. This is because I believe that any discussion of international justice must take seriously the character of relations among states, and this has been a weakness in much of the normative literature to date. After all, it is governments that sign treaties and agreements, impose sanctions and boycotts, and make war and peace, and it is governments that—for good or for bad—are ultimately accountable for their actions at home and abroad.

To be sure, much can be done to ease the plight of the poor and the excluded even in the context of an unjust international system, and I have no doubt that individuals, operating alone or more powerfully in groups such as nongovernmental organizations, can make a positive difference. Having said that, I would assert—indeed, I will try to show—that governments can feasibly build a fairer world that improves each nation's chances for sustained growth, which remains the single best instrument we know for durably improving the lives of those millions who are poor and excluded. Demonstrating that proposition—that a fairer international economy is possible—is the major burden of this book, and in the following sections I develop the theory that motivates my argument.

Liberal Internationalism and Economic Justice: An Introduction

The liberal internationalist perspective that I elaborate builds on a perspective that Charles Beitz has labeled "social liberalism."[31] Social liberals hold that international justice is built upon two distinct social compacts: first, a domestic compact, which provides societies with their basic principles of distributive justice; and second, an international compact, which provides states with the "background conditions" for the pursuit of their national welfare objectives.

At the international level, therefore, social liberals adopt a "statist" approach, asserting that states have ethical borders, and as such assume duties and responsibilities toward one another, however "weak" or "thin" these might be, in light of the absence of effective enforcement mechanisms. In this sense, liberals may be distinguished from cosmopolitan theorists on the one hand, who hold that only individuals can be conceived of as moral agents, or globalization theorists on the other, who claim, "The nation-state is just about through as an economic unit."[32]

Many social liberals locate domestic economic justice (or injustice) in particular sorts of *outcomes*, such as rising income inequality or mass poverty; this type of analysis is often called "consequentialist" in the philosophical literature, since its main concern is with the consequences of different public policies. They therefore submit that a just domestic society would seek to eliminate or rectify such undesirable outcomes. Similarly, a just international society would be one that provides its member states with the opportunities to develop their own capabilities for escaping poverty and enjoying the fruits of sustained growth, say, through free trade policies or the provision of foreign assistance.

While I certainly agree that international injustices may be located in particular outcomes, I also emphasize the normative stance of libertarian or procedural theorists, who find justice (and injustice) in the rules and procedures that shape market relationships and transactions. I do not believe that such rules are always *sufficient* for establishing a level playing field—a soccer team from a small university hardly enjoys a "level playing field" in its contest against Real Madrid, even though the ground rules are the same for both teams—but they are *necessary* to any theory of justice and should not be overlooked.[33]

I therefore call my theory *liberal internationalist* because it is primarily concerned with nation-states and their interactions.[34] Liberal internationalists hold that something like a "society of states" has evolved over time, with its members—that is, states—gradually assuming rights and obligations with respect to a set of generally agreed-upon principles, norms, and rules. The fundamental norm that regulates the international community is respect for state sovereignty and, consequently, there is a generally accepted right to noninterference in domestic affairs.

These principles imply that the cornerstone of international justice is equality in the status of states, and this provides the basis not only for international negotiations and agreements, but for world order more generally. To be sure, such equality is fictive when placed against the distribution of power—once again, my soccer team is in no way equal to a professional club, even if we agree on the rules that define the game—and it is military power that gives world politics its fundamental structure. But as we will see in future chapters, the distribution of power does not necessarily provide a complete account of state behavior and outcomes, at least in the economic realm. Because states also have an interest in order and stability, they may forgo relative gains today in the interest of building a robust system that all participants view as being reasonably fair.

According to liberal internationalists, the few principles of international justice that exist, such as sovereignty and equality, are vital to world order, even if adherence to them is often halfhearted and inconsistent. Indeed, these principles define world politics in nontrivial ways and provide the basis for the articulation of an increasing number of rules and ever-deeper interactions, including those associated with the global economy. Liberal internationalists therefore tend to conceive of economic justice in terms of the mutually advantageous and noncoercive agreements that states reach through the process of multilateral negotiations.

The challenge that these states face in their negotiations is how to construct and maintain economic arrangements that each one of them views as being in its interest. From the realist standpoint, which holds that states must be motivated by the search for "relative" as opposed to "absolute" gains, such an arrangement is nearly impossible to achieve, since of course not every state enjoys relative gains vis-à-vis the others. As a consequence, many realist scholars of world politics have asserted that it impossible to create cooperative economic institutions in the absence of a hegemonic power.[35] Later in this chapter I will show why this view is excessively pessimistic.

In an important sense, the international community has adopted, if only rhetorically, a variant of the liberal internationalist approach to economic transactions for most of the post–World War II era. That is, the system has been largely built on the normative foundation of equality among states, and most countries have been included in the major economic regimes, such as the World Trade Organization and the International Monetary Fund. But liberal internationalists do not hold, of course, that contemporary economic arrangements among states actually create a level playing field. As Dani Rodrik reminds us, "Global economic rules are not written by Platonic rulers . . . those who have power get more out of the system than those who do not."[36] Indeed, a central normative concern of most liberal internationalist thinkers is to understand, expose, and criticize the exploitative use of power relationships among states.[37] As already noted in the preface, a just international system would be inclusive, participatory, and welfare-enhancing, meaning that it would give the smallest and poorest states greater voice in the system than they have at present. This theme will be taken up again in the following chapters.

Charles Beitz has offered what remains the deepest philosophical critique of our present international economic order from a liberal internationalist perspective.[38] Like other liberal internationalists, Beitz represents the international system as a society of states whose representatives are tasked to establish a set of just principles that are to serve as the basis for the political and economic arrangements that are to govern their interactions. By applying certain aspects of Rawls's conception of domestic justice to world politics, and to the international economy more specifically, however, he arrives at some fairly radical results.[39]

Drawing on Rawls's characterization of the "original position," Beitz has us imagine a group of representatives from rich and poor countries who are bargaining over the terms of their interactions. Since they are negotiating from behind a "veil of ignorance," unaware of their particular resource endowments, he assumes that each negotiator would be risk averse and thus fearful about his or her particular condition. He posits that "not knowing the resource endowments of their own societies . . . they would agree on a resource redistribution principle."[40] The resource redistribution principle is Beitz's rough analogue to the Rawlsian difference principle, in that its objective is to improve resource endowments in the least-advantaged country, providing what he considers to be the background conditions necessary for economic growth. And since states have no prior moral claim to the resources located on their territory, patterns of inequality and poverty that result from an international system that does not redistribute such resources will be unjust. (Ironically, in *The Law of Peoples*, John Rawls rejects this by asserting that it is a country's institutions, not its resources, that provide the necessary background conditions for growth; in support of this he cites the literature on the "natural resource curse," which shows that countries rich in oil and minerals generally have poor economic performance.)

Even if we accept the need for economic redistribution, it does not follow that a coerced *resource* redistribution mechanism is necessary to provide the background conditions that enable states to achieve sustained development. In the interest of constructing a "realistic utopia," or providing a politically feasible mechanism for building a fairer world, we would do well to remember that welfare-reducing policies should be avoided.[41] Fortunately, a resource redistribution mechanism exists that is welfare-enhancing for all participants, and it is called free trade.

This claim on behalf of free trade as a welfare-enhancing redistributive mechanism is based on the thesis of economic convergence. Most countries are abundant in certain factors of production relative to other countries. China, for example, is relatively abundant in labor compared to Sweden, but Sweden is relatively abundant in capital as compared to China. When China and Sweden trade, they are actually redistributing their relative endowments of labor and capital, with Sweden receiving some labor from China (as embodied in imports of labor-intensive goods) and China receiving some capital from Sweden (as embodied in imports of Sweden's capital-intensive goods). Further, to the extent that China started trading with Sweden (and other advanced industrial countries) from a less-developed economic level, its rate of economic growth should actually exceed Sweden's over a relevant time horizon, as it reallocates its domestic resources to their most efficient use, attracts investment that seeks a high return, and imports the latest technology and management know-how. Indeed, free trade may be viewed as a uniquely suited instrument for promoting international economic justice, for the very reason that it bolsters the growth of the least-advantaged regions in a manner that is welfare-enhancing for all states.

Unfortunately, there is relatively little empirical support for the proposition that globalization is promoting convergence in growth rates or incomes among nations. And many economists argue that this is because developing countries have struggled to create the "right" sorts of institutions, say, institutions that protect property rights and civil liberties. They therefore lay the blame on domestic politics and policies rather than on the character of the international system.

Consider, for example, the assertion that "countries . . . shape their own destiny," which was often made by Lawrence Summers during his tenure as US treasury secretary in the second Clinton administration.[42] That statement reflected both his theoretical and his empirical understanding of the development process. Summers had drawn from modern growth theory the lesson that domestic policies and institutions are crucial in providing the underlying conditions necessary for investment and innovation, while empirically he knew that the *divergence* in the growth trajectories of nations during the postwar era has been dramatic, especially when compared to the *convergence* that globalization theorists would have predicted. When theory and data are combined in this way, they seem to lead easily to the conclusion that the international system exercises relatively little influence over the development process, and thus the assertion that "countries . . . shape their own destiny" appears correct.

But is this really an accurate depiction of the political structures that shape global economic transactions? Are they as benign and insignificant as Summers would have us believe? A liberal internationalist would suggest that the answer to these questions is not so obvious, and in a world where wealth and power shape the terms of international exchange, tilting the playing field in one direction or another, it would hardly be shocking to find that our public policies are failing to serve the interests of those states with the least voice in the economic system.[43]

The question thus remains as to whether the international system really presents a level playing field for each and every state. It is *not* (I would argue) the end of international economic justice to equalize economic performance through coercive resource redistribution—even if that were desirable and possible—but rather to provide the background conditions that make it possible for *all* states to exercise their comparative advantage and achieve sustained growth. Such an approach to justice, I have argued, is welfare-enhancing for all. But as we will see in the next chapter, the international trade regime remains firmly tilted against developing countries in important respects. For the liberal internationalist, only once it has been leveled, so that countries that wish to enter the global economy are able to do so, can the international community claim to have fulfilled its most basic duties in justice to each and every state.

But why should states even care about building a fairer global economy? What would possibly motivate them to do so? Why would powerful states not simply exploit the weak to the greatest extent possible, as indeed they have done throughout history? In the following sections, I will try to answer these critical questions. But first, I emphasize why it is that a theory of *international* economic justice must differ in important respects from a *domestic* theory of resource allocation, since this distinction—which some would reject on moral grounds—is absolutely critical to the liberal internationalist perspective that I adopt.

On Economic Justice, Domestic and International

In political practice, as in academic scholarship, it is notable that no single model of distributive justice has yet become dominant around the world—even among liberal democracies living at "the end of history."[44] To the contrary, polities appear to maintain significant discretion over their allocative and distributive principles. To simplify an extremely rich and complex picture, we might say that the Anglo-Saxon democracies have adopted a theory of distributive justice grounded in equality of opportunity, in which societies seek to provide the background conditions (e.g., access to education and credit markets) that permit individuals to realize their talents to the best of their abilities, whereas the Scandinavian welfare states are closer to providing "equality of resources," through wage compression, social policies, labor market institutions, and highly progressive tax structures. This rich variety of distributive schemes and principles confirm J. S. Mill's assertion that the "distribution of wealth . . . depends on the laws and customs of society. The rules by which it is determined . . . are very different in different ages and countries; and might be still more different, if mankind so chose."[45]

For a theory of international economic justice, this diversity of national schemes has a critically important implication. *What it suggests is that a just international economic arrangement among sovereign states must be supportive of each of their domestic social compacts.* That is, the international economic system must be constructed so that each polity accepts it as operating to its mutual advantage. To cite once again John Ruggie's famous phrase, international economic policies must be consistent with the bargain of "embedded liberalism" that each government has struck with its own polity, the bargain that globalization will be used as an instrument for maintaining and enhancing the social contract.[46]

The reference to "embedded liberalism" will naturally lead readers to think that I am limiting my discussion of international economic justice to justice among states that the late John Rawls would have called "well-ordered."[47] But it is not my intention to be quite so restrictive. My purpose is to make the case for the minimal set of economic arrangements that a diverse collection of states might agree to, given very different definitions of what constitutes an acceptable domestic social compact.[48]

As we will see in later chapters, international tensions will undoubtedly arise between states that define their social compact differently, as in the case of labor rights, which democratic societies may value more highly than authoritarian regimes, or in the case of the prohibition on child labor, which rich countries may value more highly than poor countries in which children routinely work. And that leads to the question of how the international community can resolve such tensions in the interest of maintaining an international economic system that is participatory, inclusive, and welfare-enhancing. One answer might be to posit the establishment of some truly global or supranational authority with the power to establish minimal social norms for all countries that wish to participate in global exchange (the International Labor Organization's "core labor standards" provides a possible model), while another might be to suggest that such conflicts can be resolved only through the exercise of hegemonic or imperial power that forces a particular set of social norms on others.

The more modest position that I take here, in contrast, is that the members of the international community would find justice only in a multilateral arrangement that enables each of them to maintain their own domestic social compact, in short, that respects their sovereignty with respect to their social norms. To be sure, there may be cases in which states practice such flagrant abuses of what are widely accepted as fundamental human rights that the international community would decide to intervene with sanctions or force, but such situations will be rare, because states would have to be convinced that their intervention will be welcomed by the local population and that it could actually improve the situation on the ground. Less dramatically, states may be tempted to sanction others because of labor, environmental, or other practices they deem unacceptable, an issue we take up in some detail in the chapter on justice in labor and migration. In general, however, states will rarely intervene in order to alter domestic social arrangements elsewhere.

Now the international system has two characteristics that are essential to understanding that a theory of economic justice pitched at the level of the society of states cannot be identical to a theory that presupposes a more or less self-contained domestic polity. First, the international system is anarchic, lacking any supranational government or superior authority. Second, as noted earlier, the society of states is characterized by a diversity of national approaches to distributive justice, a diversity of domestic social compacts. This is the environment in which the members of the international community must seek to find the common ground of justice. Thomas Pogge makes this point well when he writes, "While the world can contain societies that are structured in a variety of ways . . . it cannot itself be structured in a variety of ways."[49]

In the international setting, where states bring their own domestic conceptualizations of distributive justice to the table, their own social compacts, the challenge of creating a system that each one views as being fair or of mutual advantage would seem overwhelming, and perhaps impossible to meet, at least absent a dominant or hegemonic power that imposes its rules of the game on all the actors. Lacking a central enforcement authority that has the power to coercively redistribute the planet's wealth through tax or resource transfers, so that impoverished Chad can enjoy its "fair share" (whatever that might be) of Saudi Arabia's oil bounty and Iowa's fertile farmlands, the society of states must somehow reach agreement on an economic arrangement that each of them accepts as being participatory, inclusive, and welfare-enhancing, that is, a system that operates to their mutual advantage. In the next section I try to develop such an approach.

A Theory of International Economic Justice

For international relations theorists of the realist school, cooperation among states is scarce because world politics resembles a prisoner's dilemma game. Since states are always insecure, the threat of conflict and war inevitably casts a shadow over their relations. The result is less cooperation and more conflict than states would rationally choose if their sole objective were welfare maximization. Realists therefore assert that a dominant power, a hegemon, may be necessary to overcome this tragedy by imposing order on the international system. Conversely, cooperation is unlikely to occur when the distribution of international power is characterized by multipolarity, that is, when several states possess similar levels of power resources. Under the condition of multipolarity, security will be in short supply and the logic of relative gains will predominate. The probability of achieving durable cooperation in this setting is therefore miniscule.

Does realist logic inevitably lead states toward conflict and war? The surprising answer is no. In fact, states in a multipolar system may be predicted to act in such a way as to *balance* power, so that no hegemon emerges among them. As Bruce Bueno de Mesquita and David Lalman have put it, "If there is any distinctively political theory of international politics, balance-of-power theory is it."[50] Balance-of-power theory means that any potentially warlike state should have second thoughts about pursuing an aggressive policy against its neighbors, since systemic pressures will lead other states to form an alliance to challenge it. The only *rational* outcome for dissatisfied states in the international system is either to redress their grievances through negotiation or to accept the status quo, since war or the threat of violence will always cause a balance to form against the aggressor, making its ultimate victory unlikely. For the policy maker, then, $N > SQ > W$, where N is negotiation, SQ is the status quo, and W is war. This ranking is of tremendous consequence for international relations theory, since it leads to the conclusion that *war is not an inevitable product of the anarchic structure of the international system, but is rather due to purposeful foreign policy decisions made within nation-states.*

To illustrate this point using the specific example of economic policy, let us suppose, following the theoretical approach first developed by Jack Hirshleifer, that states can generate national income either by producing it themselves on the basis of their own resources, coupled with peaceful foreign trade, or by invading other nations and seizing their resources.[51] Knowing that each potential trading state is also a potential aggressor, rational governments will seek to minimize the risk of being invaded. They can do this by acquiring weapons and building up military power, but that will lead to a costly arms race and may actually increase the risk of war, in prisoner's dilemma fashion. Alternatively, each state can seek to mollify potential adversaries by seeking to negotiate what Hirshleifer has labeled a "potential settlement region" (PSR), or a zone of peace. Within the PSR, the benefits that flow from peaceful exchange outweigh the costs associated with a violent takeover of foreign resources. *A crucial element in establishing the PSR, the zone of peace, may be the potential for mutually advantageous trade.*

But isn't the promise of economic cooperation inevitably upset by the search for relative gains? How can states strike agreements if they are uncertain as to who will gain and who will lose in the bargain? This realist critique of cooperation theory again suggests that international arrangements must reflect the preferences of a dominant power that structures the global economy in its own self-interest.

Yet there are several problems with a theory of cooperation based on the logic of exploiting only relative gains. First, the terms of trade are often uncertain. They may be in favor of Country A today, but tomorrow they could favor Country B. Indeed, the terms of trade exhibit a fair degree of stochastic or random behavior over time, making it difficult for countries to be certain that they will be "winners"—at least in a mercantilist sense—over a politically relevant time horizon.

Second, the logic of relative gains overlooks the problem of opportunity cost. Let us imagine that the United States is fearful of striking a trade agreement with China because it believes this will enable China to grow at a faster rate, making it wealthier and more powerful as a result. Although policy makers in Washington might be tempted to reject the agreement for that reason, they would also recognize that leaving China outside the economic system may have political costs as well. If rejected by Washington, Beijing might be tempted to focus its attention on regional arrangements in Asia, and to ally with others who are dissatisfied with the American-led trade regime. Over time, this trade rivalry between the United States and China could spill over into other issue areas, making the international system less stable as a result. In contrast, by locking China into the global economy and the international institutions that govern exchange, the chances for maintaining a more peaceful and prosperous world would increase.

We are now getting closer to an ethical theory of international relations, one that is grounded in the policy *choices* that states make. If governments know, for example, that peace is more likely when trade expectations are high, and that war is more likely when they are low, this suggests that they can shape the international environment in which they exist, for better or for worse.[52] They can act in such a way as to promote a peaceful world, by increasing trade with one another. As Robert Keohane has written, "Without altering the basic structure of anarchy, governments can make the world safer, or more dangerous, through the strategies they follow."[53]

On what basis would this expansion of commerce take place? Traditionally, trade agreements—and international agreements more generally—have relied on what Keohane has called "specific reciprocity," referring to "situations in which specified partners exchange items of equivalent value in a strictly delimited sequence."[54] In trade negotiations, for example, countries offer up tariff concessions of equal value in the quest for a deal, with the Europeans opening their markets to one billion dollars of American exports if the United States does exactly the same. The game-theoretic strategy of "tit for tat" provides an example of specific reciprocity, and its power in promoting cooperative outcomes should not be underestimated. As Robert Axelrod demonstrated in *The Evolution of Cooperation*, tit for tat maximizes payoffs to the players in an iterated as opposed to a one-shot prisoner's dilemma game. Since trading relations are likely to be iterated, specific reciprocity would appear to be a sound strategy for the players to adopt, and indeed it figures prominently in the international trade regime that is institutionalized in the World Trade Organization.

But cooperation based on specific reciprocity should not be confused with an international arrangement that is necessarily considered just or fair or of mutual advantage. As Keohane has written, "Because reciprocity implies returning ill for ill as well as good for good, its moral status is ambiguous."[55] An equivalent nuclear exchange may provide a good example of specific reciprocity, but it could hardly be considered an arrangement of mutual advantage.

Further, and of greater consequence from our perspective, equivalent exchange may simply be unfair in a world of unequal state actors. Imagine a trade regime based only on specific reciprocity. Country A will offer up, say, one hundred million dollars of tariff reductions to its trading partners in the World Trade Organization if Countries B, C, and D do the same. But if Country A is, for example, the United States of America, and Country B is Bangladesh, specific reciprocity will either fail as a formula or provide fewer benefits to each party than would be the case under an alternative arrangement. Following Keohane, I call that alternative approach to negotiation "diffuse reciprocity." In the multilateral trade rounds, it is generally known as "relaxed reciprocity," or the provision of benefits to developing countries that are not fully reciprocated.

Keohane explains that under "diffuse reciprocity . . . the definition of equivalence is less precise, one's partners may be viewed as a group rather than as particular actors, and the sequence of events is less narrowly bounded. Obligations are important. *Diffuse reciprocity involves conforming to generally accepted standards of behavior*" (italics added).[56]

In policy terms, the notion of diffuse reciprocity could mean that countries exchange concessions on the basis of their relative economic size, as opposed to equivalent exchanges of equal value. In short, diffuse reciprocity suggests that "special and differential" treatment for certain states, particularly those that are relatively poor and underdeveloped, may be required as part of a just trading order, as I will elaborate in the next chapter, on justice in trade. But it is only by incorporating some notion of diffuse reciprocity that a global economy can be built that is truly inclusive and participatory; under strict tit-for-tat reciprocity, in contrast, some countries will simply be excluded from the negotiations (even if they might enjoy benefits from it).

Keohane stresses that unbalanced economic relations need not be considered "an unsatisfactory basis for long-term relationships." In support of this view, he cites the work of the anthropologist Marshall Sahlins, who has shown that among "primitive" tribes "a measure of imbalance sustains the trade partnership, compelling as it does another meeting."[57] In a similar vein, Keohane suggests that "in the world political economy, international regimes make temporary imbalances feasible, since they create incentives (in the form partly of obligations) to repay debts."[58] Again, it is the *iterated* nature of the social arrangement that helps promote rules and outcomes that are viewed as just by the trade regime's participants.

Why would great powers adopt a policy of diffuse or relaxed reciprocity in which they negotiate with and provide a level of benefits to smaller, weaker states that may not be returned in full? The answer is because the resulting international structure is likely to be more robust, more stable, as a result. World politics is full of uncertainty, and at some point small, dissatisfied powers might seek to alter the status quo. Psychological studies of violent behavior have asserted that "the idea of justice or fairness may be more centrally related to attitudes toward violence than are feelings of deprivation. It is the perceived injustice underlying the deprivation that gives rise to anger or frustration."[59] Relatedly, Donald Puchala and Raymond Hopkins have written, "The degree of bias may make a considerable difference in a regime's durability. . . . 'Fairer' regimes are likely to last longer, as are those that call for side payments to disadvantaged participants. . . . Furthermore, it can make a difference whether the norms of a regime *permit movement between the ranks of the advantaged and disadvantaged*" (italics added).[60]

The legal theorists Francesco Parisi and Nita Ghei provide, from a game-theoretic perspective, a rationale for why the norm of diffuse reciprocity can provide a stable basis for cooperation. They examine a game setting in which players "undertake repeated transactions in a stochastic game." What this means is that there is an element of randomness attached to possible outcomes, or "role reversal" in which, say, State A might be a winner in one round of play but a loser in a subsequent round. This is not to argue that world politics is stochastic in exactly the same sense—most states that are "on top" today will still be there tomorrow—but the uncertainty that resides with the system leads states to act prudently, particularly when the price associated with prudent behavior (e.g., by incorporating small nations into the trade regime) is fairly low.[61]

Under these stochastic or random conditions, "a high probability of future interaction is more likely to increase the expected payoff from cooperation." Specifically, stochastic reciprocity suggests that "an agent cooperates, not in expectation of a specific reciprocal reward, but some general reciprocal return in the future."[62] Examining the international trade regime, Keohane recognized a similar pattern when he asserted, "States in reciprocal relationships with one another often do not have identical obligations."[63]

As already mentioned, stochastic uncertainty causes states to act prudently, to behave cautiously with respect to the future course of world politics, and it encourages them to buy options against the possibility of future conflict. If a group of states is dissatisfied with the status quo, they might at some point seek to revise or overthrow it. A prudent state will therefore try to ensure that potentially dissatisfied states also view the status quo arrangement as being to their mutual advantage. Instead of adopting maximizing behavior in their international relations, great powers may come to recognize that the strategic use of coercion or force carries its own risks, particularly as it could catalyze a backlash by smaller states. *We will see in the next chapter, on justice in trade, that the outcomes of international trade negotiations are not neatly explained with reference to the distribution of power.* There is a significant "residual" that seems to emerge from a concern with achieving a "fair" or "equitable" outcome, in which each member state believes that the deal that was struck took its particular interests into account.

Political scientists have long hypothesized that, in many settings, noncoercive arrangements are likely to be more robust and less costly to maintain than policies that rely on the use of coercion or force.[64] Henry Kissinger put this sentiment well when he wrote that "agreement on shared values inhibits the desire to overthrow the world order."[65] Andrew Hurrell makes a similar point when he argues, "A great deal of the struggle for political power is the quest for authoritative control that avoids costly and dangerous reliance on brute force and coercion."[66] As usual, E. H. Carr said it best when he wrote, "Those who hope to profit most by [a political] order can in the long run only hope to maintain it by making sufficient concessions . . . to those who profit by it least."[67] In other words, there is power in moral reasoning.[68]

Again, a central finding of this line of analysis is that, far from discouraging international cooperation, uncertainty about the future course of world politics may actually encourage it! That is hardly an original observation; Thomas Schelling made it years ago when he described how agents use "focal points" in the presence of uncertainty.[69] As Barbara Koremenos, Charles Lipson, and Douglas Snidal have pointed out, states face "uncertainty about the state of the world," and they correctly intuit that this uncertainty "may . . . make cooperation easier."[70]

Modern game theory, building on models such as the "ultimatum game" (UG) and the stochastic game cited earlier, has made increasing use of uncertainty as an explanation for observed behaviors and outcomes. Under the one-shot, two-person UG, a Proposer (P) and a Respondent (R) have the opportunity to divide a sum of money. P makes an offer to R, who can either accept it or reject it. If R accepts the offer, P and R divide the money according to P's proposal. If R rejects the offer, however, both P and R must walk away from the table empty-handed, so that neither of them wins any money at all.

The classic, rational actor model of *homus economicus* would lead us to predict that P would make R a lopsided distributive offer of, say, 99/1; that is, P would offer R 1 unit, while keeping 99 units to herself. For the profit-maximizing agents in this one-shot game, 1 > 0 so both P and R are made better off even by this "egoistic" division. Maximization strategies, therefore, lead to very unequal divisions of the pie.

But experimental economists, repeating the UG in a variety of countries and under a variety of conditions, have observed a puzzling result. As Nowak, Page, and Sigmund report, "Obviously, rational responders should

accept even the smallest positive offer, since the alternative is getting nothing. Proposers, therefore, should be
able to claim almost the entire sum. In a large number of
human studies, however, conducted with different incentives in different countries, the majority of proposers offer
40 to 50 percent of the total sum; and about half of all
respondents reject offers below 30 percent."[71] The experimental economists Ernst Fehr and Simon Gachter describe R's rejection of P's offer as an example of "negative
reciprocity"; that is, an offer that is perceived by R to be
unfair is answered with rejection.[72] In contrast, fair offers
by P and their subsequent acceptance by R provide an
example of what they call "positive reciprocity."

Researchers have drawn several significant findings
from the ultimatum game, each of which finds support
in the present study.[73] First, Ps adopt moral reasoning or
other-regarding behavior out of their self-interest. Proposers who do not care about what others think must
nonetheless fear rejection of an "unfair" offer by R and
the absence of any payoff whatsoever. The adoption of
other-regarding preferences is therefore efficiency enhancing to the extent that it leads to an agreement and
thus an increase in welfare for both of the agents.

Second, the Proposer's concern with achieving an equitable or fair result arises in part from *uncertainty* about
how R will respond to its offer. If P knows that R will
willingly accept a greedy offer, P will be much more inclined to propose a lopsided division. Not knowing R's
response *ex ante*, P offers the amount it intuitively considers to be fair; more on this later.

Intriguingly, the game-theoretic setting described earlier, in which agents must make decisions about their economic interactions in the face of stochastic uncertainty,

also reminds us of the Rawlsian model of decision making with respect to a society's "basic institutions" or social contract. It will be recalled that Rawls's "original position" imagines a group of representative individuals who meet from behind a veil of ignorance, only knowing that they are expected to create enduring principles for their social interactions and institutions. These self-interested individuals may be expected to reach agreements that are ultimately in the collective interest because they imagine the changing life circumstances that could confront them or their children; in short, they must confront stochastic uncertainty and the possibility of role reversal, whereby a healthy person becomes ill or a rich person becomes poor. Keohane does not cite Rawls but makes a similar point when he writes of cooperation under diffuse reciprocity, "In such international regimes, actors recognize that a 'veil of ignorance' separates them from the future but nevertheless offer benefits to others on the assumption that they will redound to their own advantage in the end."[74]

The concept of diffuse reciprocity, of unequal exchange, is also consistent in important respects with Rawls's "difference principle," or the notion that just societies should maximize the life chances of those who are least advantaged. As Rawls says of this principle, it "expresses a conception of reciprocity. It is a principle of mutual benefit. . . . The social order can be justified to everyone, and in particular to those who are least favored; and in this sense it is egalitarian."[75] Notably, for Rawls the difference principle is crucial to social stability. Similarly, the concept of diffuse reciprocity in the global economy must take into account the resources and capabilities of each and every state, including those that are least advantaged.

By drawing on the concept of diffuse reciprocity we can see how it is possible that rational egoists, in the absence of some external enforcement mechanism, may nonetheless be able to establish among themselves "conventions," which are "forms of agreement that . . . depend upon the general consent or recognition of the society at large, rather than the formal recognition of a sovereign authority."[76] As David Lewis famously argued, conventions are built through the establishment of precedents. That is, the way in which agents behave toward one another in period 1 will influence their actions in period 2.[77] If agents behave well in period 1, we may expect that they will behave well in period 2. If they behave badly, we may expect more of the same and respond accordingly. Exchange based on diffuse reciprocity thus becomes the basis for international economic interactions, as states recognize that strictly equivalent exchange does not provide a robust basis for mutually advantageous agreements, especially in the face of stochastic uncertainty.[78]

Nations that interact on the basis of diffuse reciprocity and that view their transactions as being repeated or iterated, will enjoy a much wider scope for mutually beneficial international cooperation.[79] And unlike the international setting suggested by realist theory—in which states are always tempted to cheat on the agreements they have made and thus need an outside enforcer—this cooperation need not be imposed by a dominant power. Instead, it may be established by self-interested actors that seek to maximize their joint surplus, in the same way that early institutions designed to support long-distance trading—which proved quite durable—were established based on a nongovernmental system of sanctions among the traders themselves.[80]

International Economic Justice as Equality of Opportunity

International justice is "thin" at best. Its terms are generally vague, and to the extent it produces obligations, these are difficult to enforce. Governments routinely make pledges of all kinds—to increase foreign aid, to reduce pollution, to limit arms sales—that they fulfill only halfheartedly, if at all. Still, we have seen that even in this hostile environment, states may, out of self-interest, seek agreements that are generally viewed as "fair" or "other-regarding."

Because states are unlikely to reduce their own welfare in order to improve the welfare of others, it is dubious that a principle of justice qua "equality of resources"—as Charles Beitz, among others, has advocated—would find much political resonance among the members of the society of states, however desirable it might be from the perspective of moral philosophy. States are often happy to trade their resources to other states, but they are usually less willing to give them away for free. What model of distributive justice, then, is consistent with a world in which little generosity can be expected?

One alternative is provided by the principle of "equality of opportunity," specifically, the opportunity to achieve the world's average rate of growth. Whether a government chooses to pursue that goal will depend on domestic factors; some polities, for example, may choose less growth and more leisure. This section elaborates on that perspective, which will be further developed in the subsequent empirical chapters.

In order to appreciate the power of an equal opportunity approach to international economic justice, we must spend a moment recalling growth *theory* and its import for the society of states. For generations, economic historians have proposed that developing countries will grow *faster* than rich countries, with a tendency toward catch-up in terms of per capita income levels; "this catch-up phenomenon is referred to as *convergence*" (emphasis in original).[81] Convergence can occur along several different pathways, but one of the most promising is via technology transfer, which comes through trade and foreign direct investment. As a trio of economists has reported, "virtually all growth regressions include a catch-up term that is generally rationalized as capturing international technology transfers."[82]

We will see in the following chapters that international trade and investment provide states with an opportunity to reach the world's average growth path while increasing social welfare, and thus free trade will likely have a prominent place in any discussion of international economic justice. To be sure, as already noted, countries may not seek high growth rates, choosing instead different social compacts with different values and trade-offs, or they may simply lack the political will to build the institutions needed to sustain growth. *Still, what the society of states can plausibly do is to make it possible for each country to achieve the world's growth rate through free trade and other complementary policies.* Again, this approach is politically feasible because it is welfare-increasing rather than welfare-reducing, in contrast to the equality of resources position. It is in this sense that, following John Roemer, we associate policies that promote free trade with "equality of opportunity."[83]

It is critical to emphasize that equality of opportunity is fully consistent with the concept of diffuse reciprocity described in the previous section, or an international system grounded in maximizing the economic opportunities of the least advantaged or poorest states, in the same way that affirmative action may be viewed as consistent with a domestic notion of equal opportunity. This is because a trading system based solely on equivalent exchange of reciprocal "concessions" would simply not be capable of promoting equal opportunity; in such a system, smaller or poorer states would have little to offer those that were wealthier or less dependent on international commerce for growth. States, like domestic societies, will adopt equal opportunity policies in part because of stochastic uncertainty about the future course of world politics, or the concern that someday a dissatisfied country, or group of dissatisfied countries, could choose to band together to overthrow the status quo.

As Roemer and his colleague Humberto Llavador put it:

> Primary to the conception of equal opportunity is the distinction between two attributes of the "individuals" among whom opportunities for some objective will be equalized—their "circumstances" and their "effort." The circumstances of an individual (our individuals will be "countries") are attributes that influence the degree to which it can achieve the objective in question (for us, a growth rate), and which are beyond its control, or are not changeable in the short run. In contrast, "effort" refers to actions the individual takes, which also influence the degree to which it achieves the objective, but which are deemed to be "within its control" or are changeable in the short run. . . . *[T]o equalize opportunities means to level the playing field, where the troughs and gulleys in the field are the disadvantages countries suffer . . . due to poor circumstances. Once the playing field is leveled by application of a judicious policy, then*

the difference in outcomes will be due only to differences in efforts." [italics added][84]

Within the framework of international economic justice, these national circumstances can be offset through the combination of free trade and foreign aid to promote open markets; having done that, domestic policies will then play a decisive role in determining growth rates.

To be sure, there are many practical difficulties associated with the removal of the economic and political barriers to national attainment. Just as individuals may face a multitude of roadblocks to success—their family background, neighborhood, income bracket, and so forth—countries may face barriers in terms of geography, natural resources, a lack of savings, or a lack of human capital. Under an equality of opportunity theory of international economic justice, the society of states must seek to remove the barriers to development created by their policies so that no state believes that the international "system" has conspired against it in such a way as to deny its growth prospects. Through free trade and foreign aid, for example, the international community does what it reasonably can to help countries to attain their highest growth path.

Free trade is essential to equal opportunity because it helps countries to overcome resource shortages by making available, in the international marketplace, goods and services in which they do not hold a comparative advantage, or makes available more goods than they can produce domestically. Further, trade, investment, and technology transfer can boost domestic growth rates. Foreign assistance can help countries overcome "bottlenecks" that may prohibit them from entering the global economy to the fullest extent. Conversely, trade barriers or discriminatory customs unions undermine equality of opportunity, making it more difficult for states to do as well as they can. I treat justice in trade and justice in aid in considerable detail in the following chapters.

Conclusion: Toward Justice among States

In this book, I endow economic relations among states with something like a moral character.[85] The approach follows closely the one taken by Hedley Bull in *The Anarchical Society*, and in many respects the present work may be seen in the context of the "English School" of international relations theory. Bull wrote, "Because states are the main agents or actors in world politics, ideas of interstate justice provide the main content of everyday discussion of justice in world affairs. Every state maintains that it has certain rights and duties that are not merely legal in character but moral: it contends that its policy is just in the sense of being morally correct *and demands equality or fairness of treatment as between itself and other states*" (italics added).[86]

My position, then, is that justice among nations may be said to exist and is a relevant category for theoretical analysis. Although I do not deny the pull of cosmopolitanism, I believe that this perspective can be made policy-relevant only in the context of a more peaceful and prosperous international system. When states deny one another the possibility of shaping their own destinies, it becomes much more difficult to achieve cosmopolitan objectives. In an important sense, cosmopolitan and liberal internationalist theories must find common cause if they are to promote greater global justice.

But how can states, locked in the anarchic realm of world politics, advance the cause of international economic justice? And why would they do so when the instruments of brute force are always available to them?

In this chapter I have sketched a theory of international economic justice, grounded in the self-interest of states that interact in the context of an anarchic and insecure political environment. Concern with the stability of international arrangements, combined with the stochastic uncertainty associated with the global economy (and world politics more generally), makes it prudent for states to negotiate agreements that all members of the international community, including smaller and weaker nations, find reasonably fair or just. In the absence of these considerations of fairness and justice, states would have greater motivation to revise or overturn, perhaps violently, the status quo. By providing a level playing field on which states can do as well as they are able—through trade, investment, and limited access to foreign aid—the members of the society of states seek to ensure a more stable and prosperous world.

That summarizes the theory of international economic justice that I defend in this book. In the following chapters, we will have a chance to test it against the case studies of trade, aid, labor, and investment. As we will see, ideas of justice and fairness have crept into each of these issue areas, even in a world where the distribution of wealth and power remains the major determinant of international relations. The presence of these ideas is suggestive of the recognition among policy makers that durable and robust systems of international cooperation cannot be reliably built upon the threat of violence alone.

2

FAIRNESS IN TRADE

Probably the single most effective action that the
industrial countries could implement to alleviate
the terrible problem of poverty in many developing countries would be to open, unilaterally,
markets to imports from those countries.
—Alan Greenspan

Free trade is widely held by economists to promote
global efficiency and growth, but a rising chorus
of voices is asserting that it has not done much to
help developing countries and the poor, at least given the
current structure of the international trade regime. Are
these accusations true? Is the international trade regime
tilted against the weakest states and the most vulnerable
persons within them?

In the previous chapter, we saw that international trade
has been charged with contributing to negative economic
outcomes such as rising poverty and income inequality
within and among nations. The trade regime has also
been criticized in terms of its rule-making procedures,
which appear to favor the rich states and their multinational corporations. For example, the prominent nongovernmental organization Oxfam has stated, "The problem
is not that international trade is inherently opposed to the
needs and interests of the poor, but that the rules that
govern it are rigged in favor of the rich."[1] The Harvard

economist Dani Rodrik has expressed a similar sentiment, because that "Global economic rules are not written by Platonic rulers. . . . [T]hose who have power get more out of the system than those who do not."[2]

These criticisms force us to compare the theoretical arguments for free trade that economists like to make with the international trade regime as it actually exists in practice. It also leads us to ponder what a fairer trade regime might look like. Do we live in the best of all possible worlds, or can normative theory help point the way toward positive change?

It is worthwhile to emphasize that, in the economics literature at least, free trade has traditionally been defended on both positive and normative grounds. As a body of positive theory, international economics holds that the freeing of trade and capital flows leads to an efficient allocation of the world's scarce resources, generating greater output and consumption than would be possible under protectionism. As a normative doctrine, it claims in utilitarian fashion that free trade also makes for good policy, since more output and consumption is preferable to less. Further, international relations theorists (and practitioners) have long held that free trade contributes to peace, and some economists would agree that this is its single most important contribution to the society of states.[3] As Kenneth Boulding once wrote, "The case for free trade has always been a moral one."[4]

But utilitarian economic theory is relatively silent on the question of how these gains from trade ought to be distributed both within and among nations.[5] Some utilitarians even assert that this is one of the doctrine's great strengths. In the words of the Nobel Prize–winning economist John Hicks, "If measures making for efficiency are to have a fair chance, it is extremely desirable that they should be freed from distributive complications as much as possible."[6]

Such a statement amounts to wishing away politics, for it is these "distributive complications" that lie at the heart of controversies over economic justice. Accordingly, these are the complications that I will address in this chapter. Specifically, I seek to provide a normative assessment of the international trade regime—its rules and procedures, and the outcomes that these generate for states. I thus seek to establish whether the trade regime is a structure that each participant can accept as being one that is participatory, inclusive, and welfare-enhancing. As we will see, the picture is a mixed one: while the overall structure of the trade regime is discriminatory in important respects, ideas of fairness have nonetheless played a surprising role in shaping actual trade negotiations.

In order to bring some formal structure to the theoretical problem of justice in trade, the chapter opens with the hypothetical establishment of a basic trade regime. The first challenge that the negotiators of such a regime will encounter is to forge a set of rules for international trade that each of them considers fair. After considering the rules and procedures that would shape this hypothetical trade agreement, we then turn to the real world of recent trade negotiations. Despite their mercantilist elements, these agreements cannot be neatly understood in terms of either the efficiency (i.e., welfare-maximizing) or political economy (i.e., vote-maximizing) models of policymaking. Instead, it appears that trade negotiators have also been motivated by a notion of justice in which each state contributes its "fair share" to an outcome that liberalizes and increases world trade for all.

We then turn to the more specific problem of developing countries within the international trading system. For most of the postwar era, the structure of the trade regime did not encourage developing countries to have much of a voice in the various trade rounds, and as a consequence they were left out of the decision-making process; in short, the trade regime was neither inclusive nor participatory. To be sure, a variety of programs were adopted unilaterally by the great economic powers in the economic "interest" of developing countries, such as the "generalized system of preferences" (GSPs) and "special and differential status" (S&D) with respect to trade obligations, and in some respects these can be viewed as being consistent with a theory of justice as fairness. But they are not really examples of diffuse reciprocity, meaning that developing countries assumed very little or no obligation at all under this framework. That is a failure that should be corrected in future rounds of trade talks.

This failure is exemplified by the case study that we will treat later in the chapter, which concerns intellectual property rights for pharmaceutical products. In recent years, developing countries and their industrialized-world advocates within nongovernmental organizations have charged that the intellectual property provisions of the trade regime make it costly—too costly—for poor countries to receive vital medicines to meet the AIDS epidemic and other public health challenges. Accordingly, activists have argued that pharmaceutical companies and industrial world governments should make funds available, or offer drugs at little or no cost (or alternatively, to open the market to cheap generic drugs), so that poverty would not be a barrier to drug access. These issues are clearly problems of distributive justice, which political theory should help us to address.

Finally, we turn to the issue of compensation for the "losers" from economic opening. Rising unemployment for industrial workers, for example, *could* be an outcome of increasing openness and this might be disruptive to the domestic social compact. Does that mean that free trade is inconsistent with international economic justice?

The answer is no. For the same reason that we would not seek to halt technological change solely because of its distributive consequences within societies, we would not want to stop free trade. Still, societies must knit social safety nets to help those displaced by the policy shift to greater openness. If domestic societies lack the wherewithal to fashion these safety nets, as could be the case in some developing countries, they may seek help from the international community, a case we will make in chapter 3, on justice in foreign aid.

Free Trade and International Justice

To begin our analysis, let us imagine a group of hypothetical negotiators, representatives of their national governments, who are haggling over the terms of an international trade agreement. At the outset of the talks, the member states commit themselves to accepting the outcome of the process, but of course a group of them, a coalition, could decide to quit the negotiations at any time and pursue their own agreement. Elaborating on a game-theoretic model of Rawlsian bargaining initially developed by Howe and Roemer, we can say that free trade is at the core of this bargaining session, this game, if and only if "there is no coalition which can better the lot of all its members by exercising its withdrawal option" during the negotiations.[7]

To put this somewhat differently, we might think of the core of the game in terms of the opportunity cost facing a coalition as it contemplates withdrawal from the international agreement that is being negotiated.[8] If a coalition of states of type N is certain that it can obtain a larger bundle outside the framework of the agreement, then it would have good reason to reject it. In short, we can safely assume participation in the international trade regime must serve the interests of each negotiator better than nonparticipation.

Let us now pursue the negotiations as they unfold, beginning with the simplest model imaginable. We will then progressively introduce some "real world" complications. In building the model we make the following key assumptions:

1. The actors are representatives of sovereign nation-states.

2. There are two types of states, N and S, which are, respectively, "big," wealthy, and capital-intensive (N), and "small," poor, and labor-intensive (S). Capital is assumed to be a mobile factor of production, while labor is immobile. There are constant returns to scale (an assumption that will be relaxed later when we discuss increasing returns). Unlike the Rawlsian original position, we will assume that the negotiators know whether they are representing N or S.

3. The actors are familiar with the standard theories of international trade, including the arguments for and against various types of protection.

4. The societies are well ordered from a Rawlsian perspective, meaning that any problems that economic open-

ing may create for the domestic social compact in terms of
unemployment or changes in income distribution can be
settled according to the society's principles of economic
justice. These policy responses could include, for example,
lump-sum transfers to compensate for the losses that international trade may create for certain groups, access to education and training, or other social safety net programs.

*On the basis of these assumptions, the negotiators in this setting
are solely concerned with establishing just economic arrangements at the international level.*

For illustrative purposes, let us launch our hypothetical
negotiations by considering the most basic array of possible international economic schemes. These are as follows:

a. Both N and S adopt free trade.
b. N adopts protection, S free trade.
c. S adopts protection, N free trade.
d. Both N and S adopt protection.

The question before each negotiator in this first round
of talks is therefore whether to be a free trader or a protectionist. The answer is easy for countries of type S.
They are price takers who cannot influence the terms of
trade and must therefore find free trade to be their first-
best outcome. Thus, for S, a > c.

And what are the preferences of countries of type N?
For these "big" countries, an optimum tariff would in fact
be preferable to free trade, since they are price makers
who can extract "rents" from the international system.
Thus, for N, b > a.

But negotiators from N might hesitate before imple-
menting that trade policy. For the problem that countries
of type N will face is that, in exercising optimum tariffs,
they must be prepared for economic or even violent re-

taliation by other states.[9] Any country S that faces a tariff wall established by one or more Ns will have a powerful incentive to create a trading bloc or customs union with countervailing market power. That would make all the trading partners worse off than they were before, in prisoner's dilemma fashion.[10] As we saw in the previous chapter, even big countries might prefer to keep small countries in the game instead of leaving them dissatisfied and outside the system.

Over the long term, the threat of S's withdrawal from the trading system might have undesirable consequences for stability and prosperity that N would rather not risk. Because of that uncertainty over the future course of world politics, N will act prudently, seeking to buy an option on good relations with S by building a "potential settlement region" with it, which increases S's trade expectations and makes the prospects for a stable trading arrangement between N and S more likely. That, in turn, would lengthen the shadow of the future and provide even further incentives to maintain their cooperative undertaking. This is consistent with an approach to international trade that is both realist and moral. The optimum tariff, in contrast, would lack robustness because of its failure to contribute to stable international relations. It is notable in this context that the United States refrained from adopting optimum tariff policies at the end of World War II, when the temptation would have been strongest from a purely economic perspective. *The optimum tariff therefore lies outside the core of the game*, and there is no trade policy that is better for any country, including the least advantaged S, than free trade.

Another important result associated with free trade that the negotiators would undoubtedly consider is that when countries trade, there is a tendency (in theory) for factor prices to converge.[11] Indeed, the factor price equalization (FPE) theorem *would seem to neatly satisfy the Rawlsian "difference principle" on an international level, as it suggests that labor in S—that is, the least advantaged persons in the poorest countries—would be among the "winners" from a free trade regime.* And even without the assumption of FPE, one can still argue from a cosmopolitan perspective that free trade is especially good for the poor, because it tends to lower the prices of basic consumption goods such as food and clothing, on the one hand, while promoting economic growth, on the other.[12]

But negotiators from S would certainly remind their colleagues from N that FPE makes powerful and unrealistic assumptions, most notably that technology is identical in all countries. That is palpably not true, and since countries do not, in fact, have equal access to technology, but rather innovation appears to be highly concentrated in countries of type N, these states will likely enjoy higher incomes than those of type S. Further, because of this technology gap, states of type S will fail to "catch up" or enjoy economic convergence, and may even fall behind. Let us therefore imagine a world of increasing returns, in which scale economies in technological development lead to the creation of quasi monopolies. It is difficult to believe that this arrangement can be defended as one of mutual advantage that also serves the interests of states of type S. Charles Beitz, for example, has argued that "Because states have . . . varying access to technology, even 'free' trade can lead to increasing international distributive inequalities."[13]

Beitz's assertion is motivated by the seemingly reasonable position that, given the differences in technological capacity between N and S in the presence of increasing returns, N might be tempted to exercise its monopoly power by withholding such technology from the international marketplace or by charging high rents for it. But there are several problems that N must contend with before it adopts that policy approach.

First, it must be certain that it can identify and employ the appropriate policy instruments that are best suited to meeting its income-maximizing objectives. If, for example, it seeks to protect or subsidize those sectors where increasing returns obtain, it must not then extend protection to other import-competing industries as well. For reasons of domestic political economy, however, it may be difficult to engage in such precise industrial targeting; to put this in other words, it is difficult to be just a little bit of a protectionist.

Second, as we have already noted in discussing the optimum tariff, N must be sure that it will not face tariff retaliation—or more violent forms of conflict—from other states that seek "fair" access to foreign technology. The costs of a possible conflict must be weighed against the benefits that monopoly power might bring. As a result of these two factors, "economists today have returned in hordes to free trade" despite the presence of increasing returns, and we might therefore expect N to do so as well.[14]

S, however, must still be worried by N's intentions. From the perspective of S, the prospect of living in a world of increasing returns makes it seems reasonable to propose that a global technology pool be established to ensure that all countries would have equal access to the fruits of human creation, a radical redistribution scheme for technology. It is significant that some developing countries have called for such common technological pools in the past, as with their demand in the 1970s for the establishment of a new international economic order. The current debate over the role of intellectual property rights within the context of multilateral trade agreements, which is discussed in greater detail later in this chapter, is also fundamentally about distributive justice with respect to technologies such as patented medicines.

This demand for a common technological pool would require careful study. And our analysis might well lead us to caution in making such a bold proposal. The problem is that a radical redistribution of technology to states that have not paid for it—that is, treating technology like a quasi-public good—must decrease the returns to innovation, undermining the incentive to invest in the very research and development that spurs technological change and economic growth in the first place. If technology were made freely available, "little innovation would ever take place," and that would be harmful not only to N but to S as well.[15]

The reason why N's potential failure to innovate could be harmful to S is for the simple reason that S may ultimately depend on technology transfer from N for its economic development and growth. Following a model developed by Paul Krugman, let us assume a world in which the only goods produced by these states are, respectively, "new goods" and "old goods."[16] Country N innovates and produces new goods, which it then exports to S. As a result of the innovation process, the wages in N rise as they capture the rents associated with the new good. At first it appears that N's technological advantage increases the global disparity of income between N and S, thus making negotiators from S take seriously the possibility that some technology or income redistribution scheme, assuming for the moment that one could be agreed upon, must be preferable to the "free trade" result.

But over time, N transfers technology to S and then imports old goods from it. In the process, labor in S substitutes for labor in N, and wages in S rise accordingly. As Krugman concluded, "innovation disproportionately benefits the developed country, while technology transfer can actually make the developed country worse off."[17] With technology transfer, the terms of trade favor S, not N. This is the precise sort of "role reversal" that I discussed in chapter 1, where I argued that uncertainties associated with the terms of trade over time made cooperation based on diffuse rather than specific reciprocity appealing to countries seeking to build a legitimate and robust economic arrangement.

What are the net effects of this "bargain" in which N holds the innovative advantage over S? That is an empirical question, but we can say with confidence that the answer will ultimately depend on *national* economic policies. If N encourages innovation to a greater degree than S favors foreign direct investment and technology transfer, then N will emerge the "winner." If both adopt equally favorable domestic policies and then engage in free trade, the benefits of the innovation/transfer process should be evenly distributed. Trade enables each country to do as well as it can, but national policies and preferences may push countries along different economic trajectories and growth paths. In this way, free trade discriminates between effort and circumstance, as the "equality of opportunity" approach to justice discussed in the previous chapter would suggest.

It is also critical to emphasize the important result that N's technological advantage would in no way give it a higher long-run *growth* path than S, because trade pushes all countries toward the *"same long-run growth rate."*[18] It is *national* differences in endowments and, more critically, differences in public policies that lead to differences in incomes; but trade is indeed equalizing to the extent that it leads national growth paths to converge toward some global average.

This discussion should not be taken to imply that free trade is a "panacea for . . . inequalities," for surely, as Paul Samuelson reminded us many years ago, it is not.[19] The international system cannot make up for all the domestic shortfalls—natural and manmade—that may constrain economic development, and this leads to the "duty of assistance," which I will discuss in the next chapter. Still, the establishment of a free trade regime is hardly a trivial exercise for the international community; at least in theory; it provides the best opportunity for every state to achieve the world's long-run growth path. So much for the theory: in the next section, I take up the problem of trade negotiations in the "real world."

Trade Negotiations in the "Real World": Does Fairness Matter?

In the nitty-gritty world of trade policymaking, negotiators operate within the context of a complex political environment in which domestic and international pressures both influence the position they adopt with respect to tariff liberalization. As Robert Putnam has argued, diplomacy is a "two-level game," with a variety of interests struggling for political influence.[20]

The underlying model shaping much of our political economic analysis of trade policy is one of endogenous tariff formation, where import-sensitive companies buy trade protection from electorally sensitive politicians, who gain campaign contributions and votes in return. The higher the degree of import sensitivity, the more money firms are willing to pay for protection. Consumers, in contrast, face a tremendous collective action problem in organizing their support for free trade. Each consumer gains relatively little, and is hardly motivated to make a campaign contribution to support a free trade policy. Special interests, in contrast, have a lot more at stake, and respond accordingly.

Given the overwhelming presence of domestic political economy considerations in the making of trade policy, it is hardly surprising that discussions of justice and fairness have been notable by their absence in the relevant literature.[21] Yet this emphasis on domestic political factors leads us to overlook the collective norms that have shaped and continue to shape the trade regime; indeed, these norms may even constrain the exercise of power politics to some degree. In particular, the world trade order has been built on two norms: first, most favored nation (MFN) status, and second, reciprocity.

With MFN, "countries must treat their trading partners equally, without discrimination. Any special trade concession or favor given to one country must be extended automatically to all other GATT (WTO) members."[22] What this means is that *all* member governments of the World Trade Organization (WTO) enjoy the benefits of the trade deals that have been negotiated in the multilateral context, and no state can be excluded. When viewed from the harsh perspective of world politics, this represents a remarkable norm of behavior, and it contributes mightily to greater *inclusiveness* in the trade regime.

The norm of reciprocity within the General Agreement on Tariffs and Trade (GATT)/WTO context, in contrast, refers to the conditional nature of trade agreements, meaning that the negotiating parties, say, the United States and the European Union, will aim to achieve "broadly matching levels of restriction or openness of trade, both with respect to individual sectors and bilateral trade balance."[23] This reciprocity condition, in contrast, is essential to trade policy for "good" reasons of domestic political economy. Because politicians must weigh protectionist against export-oriented interests, they can pursue liberalization at home only when they win equivalent levels of liberalization abroad. These "concessions" to liberalize must be, in tit-for-tat fashion, more or less balanced or reciprocal. It is this norm of reciprocity that is most problematic in the context of justice as fairness, for it limits *participation* in WTO negotiations by the least developed countries.

The issue at stake is that under such a reciprocity-based system, where reciprocity is defined in terms of tit for tat or equivalent exchange, it is impossible for small economies to have much voice at the bargaining table, because their offers of market liberalization will be trivial and fail to attract much attention from the great powers. Ghana and Bangladesh simply do not have the market size to draw the interest of trade negotiators from the United States and the European Union—winning a few million dollars of market access from them is simply not worth bargaining over when scarce political capital can be deployed elsewhere. Because the developing countries have not had much voice in the reciprocal bargaining framework, they have been unable to win liberalization in the sectors of greatest importance to them—notably agriculture; more on this in the next section.

Interestingly, the reciprocity norm is featured in the preamble to the GATT but in a rather ambiguous light. The preamble reads that countries will advance the objective of lowering barriers to trade "by entering into reciprocal *and mutually advantageous* arrangements" (italics added). However, reciprocity qua equivalent exchange cannot be seen as the basis for an international trade regime that is viewed by each participant as mutually advantageous or fair. Instead, the reciprocity principle has to be "diffuse" or "relaxed," recognizing the relative bargaining power of the economy in question. The concept of reciprocity in the context of the trade regime must therefore be sensitive to the requirements of the "least advantaged" states: those lacking the human, natural, or financial resources necessary for carving out their place in the division of labor. Justice as fairness demands that their needs be met.

In fact, it appears that ideas of fairness, or of trade as a system of mutual advantage, *have* played a role in shaping the international trade regime, even if less completely than one would wish if that arrangement were to be accepted as being just. Notably, in seeking to explain the outcomes of various trade rounds over the years, economists have been puzzled to see the fairness factor at work. In a path-breaking paper, Kenneth Chan sought to explain the results of the Tokyo Round of trade negotiations that took place between 1973 and 1979. He hypothesized that a trade round could reflect *efficiency* concerns, in which the objective of the negotiators is to maximize global output, or what he called *egalitarian* or *equity* concerns, in which the countries sought an agreement that each of them considers to be fair. Based on his empirical analysis of the completed trade round, he concluded that "the major determinant" of the agreement that was reached was "the *egalitarian* nature of the solution" (italics in original).[24]

"Why," Chan asked, "are *egalitarian* considerations so important in international negotiation? A plausible explanation is that each player has (roughly) equal destructive power. Each player could easily develop an opposing 'Force,' by joining forces with some dissatisfied developing countries (or small developed countries) who were left on the 'periphery' of the negotiation."[25] We have already noted why it is that "big" countries would not exercise the optimum tariff option in a hypothetical trade negotiation, and Chan provides empirical evidence in support of that finding.

Chan also notes that the "egalitarian spirit" was reflected in the Tokyo Round declaration, which states, "To this end, co-ordinated efforts shall be made to solve in an equitable way the trade problems of all participating countries. . . . The negotiations shall be conducted on the basis of the principles of mutual advantage, mutual commitment and overall reciprocity."[26] It should be emphasized that the phrase *overall reciprocity* was used rather than *specific reciprocity*, to reflect the notion that the trade round's reciprocity could be understood only within the larger context of the society of states, with their varying capacities to offer up concessions on market access.

In a similar exercise, J. Michael Finger and his World Bank colleagues sought to understand the outcomes of bargaining in the Uruguay Round of talks the during 1980s. They hypothesized that states could be expected to adopt a negotiating posture shaped by the exigencies of domestic political economy, or what they call a mercantilist

TABLE 2.1

Concessions Received and Given During the Uruguay Round ($MM)

Country/Region	Concessions Received	Concessions Given
European Union	578,816	627,939
United States	214,791	283,580
Argentina	6,331	0
Brazil	38,037	98
Chile	3,291	0
Colombia	6,323	81
India	14,380	67,172
Indonesia	16,222	3,355
Malaysia	36,108	28,966
Mexico	960	3
Peru	1,586	58
Philippines	19,748	12,847
Sri Lanka	1,595	33
Thailand	20,564	95,953
Uruguay	772	6
Venezuela	2,051	806

Source: J. Michael Finger, Ulrich Reincke, and Adriana Castro, "Market Access Bargaining in the Uruguay Round: Rigid or Relaxed Reciprocity?" World Bank Working Paper no. 2258 (1999).

Note: Concessions received and given are calculated as the anticipated value of the tariff cuts in millions of dollars.

bargaining model, in which each state seeks to maximize *its own* economic benefit. They then evaluated this hypothesis against the actual pattern of tariff reductions that occurred. Did the United States and the European Union extract more concessions from the rest of the word than they gave up to smaller nations, as the mercantilists would predict? Or did they give up more concessions, in the name of promoting greater market access for all countries?

As table 2.1 shows, the United States and the European Union gave up far more by way of trade concessions (again meaning liberalization measures) than they received from the rest of the world. Like Chan, Finger and his colleagues also found that the trade negotiations were powerfully shaped by "a sense of fairness, of appropriate contribution."[27] In their interviews with trade negotiations, the concept of fairness that emerged was one of "sacrifice for the common good," in which industrial countries cut their tariffs by more than the amount demanded of developing countries. Further, industrial countries offered to developing states more "concessions" than they received from them.

To be sure, in neither the Tokyo nor the Uruguay Rounds did the negotiating parties, including the advanced industrial states, adopt a principle of free trade, nor can the final agreements be viewed as "fair," especially to developing countries. What Finger and his coauthors overlook is that the sectors of most importance to the developing world were largely exempted from the liberalization process, meaning that markets in the United States and the European Union (and Japan) were almost impossible to penetrate for certain commodities. As a consequence, commentators have argued that the Final Act of the Uruguay Round was "unfairly asymmetrical, especially in the leniency with which it treated agricultural and textile and clothing protection by developed countries."[28] Studies of the Uruguay Round have found that "developed countries will receive the lion's share of the welfare gains generated by the trade barrier reductions."[29] That outcome reflects wealth and power more than it does fairness.

The Uruguay Round also included an agreement on trade-related intellectual property rights (TRIPS), which has gone to the heart of disputes between the industrial and developing worlds over justice in the global

economy; accordingly, this will be discussed in a later section. As if to counterbalance all these industrialed-world
advantages, however, the round incorporated new dispute
settlement procedures that were designed to make it easier for developing countries, among others, to bring their
complaints about trade barriers before the newly created
WTO. Overall, therefore, the international trade regime
still cannot be considered as being just to all participating
countries—the reciprocal nature of the bargaining game
gives small countries relatively little voice in the negotiating process—but ideas of fairness have nonetheless ani-
mated the agreements in ways that have tempered mercantilist dictates at least to some limited degree.

Developing Countries, International Trade, and Economic Justice

At the outset of this chapter, we imagined a world of free
trade and tried to demonstrate that such an arrangement
would be to the mutual advantage of each and every state.
In the real world, however, free trade does not obtain, and
trade negotiations are driven mainly by political economy
considerations, which often require states to deliver "reciprocal" agreements based on equivalent exchange. As a
consequence, developing countries do not participate in
the trade regime as much as do industrial states, and they
do not enjoy the full benefits of market access to rich
world markets. Because they are not able to bargain over
the terms of liberalization, the sectors of greatest importance to them have remained outside the trade regime and
are heavily protected. As Harry Johnson wrote in 1967,
"In an important sense the trade policies of the developed

countries may be said to discriminate against the less developing countries."[30]

The trade regime's reliance on reciprocity qua equivalent exchange has been sharply criticized by developing countries that seek a greater role in the international economy. As an Egyptian diplomat has argued, "the basic approach underlying multilateral trade negotiations—that of granting reciprocal concessions—though seemingly rational, poses considerable difficulties for developing countries and places them at a disadvantage in the process of negotiations."[31]

Tensions between the industrial and less developed countries (LDCs) have characterized the international trading system ever since its modern origins at the end of World War II.[32] Although "more than eleven of the original twenty-three contracting parties of the GATT were developing countries, they did not effectively participate in or deem it a framework that would promote their interests."[33] It was apparent to these negotiators that trade liberalization would occur only on a quid pro quo or tit-for-tat basis, and although that may have been a sound strategy for the industrial countries, it did little to open markets for developing world exports. Further, at least two of the sectors in which developing countries possessed comparative advantage, namely agriculture and textiles, were among those most protected by the developed world.

It is thus not surprising that developing countries have expressed doubts as to whether the trade regime was designed with their economic interests in mind, that is, whether it is a system of mutual advantage. Interestingly, the concerns that they expressed during the postwar GATT talks about regime design were completely misinterpreted by the American delegate Clair Wilcox, who asserted that the LDCs had come to these discussions with the misguided idea that "wealth and income ... should be redistributed between the richer and the poor states. Upon the rich obligations should be imposed; upon the poor, privileges should be conferred. . . . The voluntary acceptance by all states of equal obligations with respect to commercial policy must be rejected as . . . a means by which the strong would dominate the weak."[34] Clearly, Wilcox did not understand how the structure of the trade regime discriminated against these developing world states.

In the early postwar years, the notion that poor nations might require anything like diffuse reciprocity or special treatment to succeed in the nascent global economy did not figure prominently in mainstream views of the development process. As John P. Lewis has written, "The classic development strategy did not require the rich countries to enter into any grandiose share-the-wealth schemes. We were able to tell ourselves that these were not only infeasible; they were unnecessary."[35] To be sure, the World Bank—an international transfer mechanism—was created at the 1944 Bretton Woods conference in order to provide some financial and technical assistance, but this was mainly in the form of country risk guarantees that, according to its articles of agreement, were designed "to promote foreign investment."

Trade did not play a significant role in the classic growth models, and to the extent that development economists thought about free trade, it was generally in critical terms. Specifically, economists such as Raul Prebisch of the United Nations argued that developing countries inevitably faced declining terms of trade for commodity exports relative to imports of manufactured goods, meaning that they would have to export more and more in order to import less and less, echoing the nineteenth-century Russian lament that "we export even though we die." The policy advice that followed from this line of analysis was that commodity exporters should build tariff walls in order to build infant industries that would provide the foundation for an economically diverse and stable economy, and indeed the GATT's article XVIII provided an opt-out for infant industry protection.[36]

It is notable, however, that some neoclassical economists disputed these assertions and the associated policy advice. Gerald Meier was particularly critical of the structuralists and their methodological foundations. Their "analytical reasoning is unconvincing," he wrote. "It is difficult to entertain seriously the argument that the slow pace of development has been due to a worsening in the terms of trade." Meier pointed to domestic rather than international factors as the root cause of slow growth. If these domestic impediments to the efficient utilization of the factors of production were removed, he was certain that trade would prove an "engine of growth."[37]

In seeking a deeper understanding of the relationship between trade and development, in 1957 the GATT appointed a wise men's committee chaired by the distinguished Harvard economist Gottfried Haberler. It concluded with a scathing condemnation of the trade policies of the industrial states, stating, "Barriers of all kinds in developed countries contributed significantly to the trade problems of developing countries." It called on the GATT to promote tariff reductions, especially on tropical products.

Further, the committee recognized that the industrial countries had adopted insidious policies of "tariff escala-

TABLE 2.2
Industrial-World Tariff Escalation

Product	Post-Uruguay Round Tariff Rates
Industrial products	
Raw materials	0.8
Semi-finished manufactures	2.8
Finished products	6.2
Tropical industrial products	
Raw materials	0.0
Semi-manufactures	3.4
Finished products	2.4
Natural resource–based products	
Raw materials	2.0
Semi-manufactures	2.0
Finished products	5.9

Source: International Monetary Fund (IMF) and World Bank, "Market Access for Developing Countries' Exports" (electronic manuscript, IMF, and World Bank, 27 April 2001), p. 23.

tion" that placed higher tariffs on, say, refined agricultural products than on crops, making it uneconomical for developing countries to invest in value-added processing technology and leaving them to rely on unstable commodity exports. Indeed, tariff escalation remains prominent today, as illustrated by table 2.2. But despite these findings, little progress would be made in reducing tariffs on agricultural products and textiles for many years, and even today the barriers to trade in these goods remain relatively high when compared to liberalization in other areas.[38]

That the status quo trade regime impeded the developing world's growth prospects became increasingly clear during the 1960s. In 1961, the United Nations Commission on Europe produced a major report titled *Europe and the Trade Needs of the Less Developed Countries*, which projected Third World exports and imports over the next twenty years. It predicted that the combination of official aid flows and earnings from exports of commodities would meet only two-thirds of developing world import requirements. The report concluded that this amount would have "to be filled by manufactures," and it proposed the establishment of a "generalized system of preferences" (GSPs), whereby developing countries would receive *better than* MFN status for tariffs, for the purpose of encouraging LDC exports.[39]

That same year, the United Nations also launched its Development Decade, setting a target for developing country growth rates of 5 percent per annum (how the United Nations thought it could realistically set a target for such growth rates is another question that we will not probe here). At the same time, the Group of 77 developing countries proposed the establishment of a new economic organization that would be more attuned to their special needs and that could give them a stronger collective voice in promoting the international policies that would help reach that target. Thus, in 1964 the United Nations Conference on Trade and Development (UNCTAD) was launched.

High on the UNCTAD agenda was lobbying on behalf of the GSP scheme. The European Union would ultimately adopt GSPs in 1971, in response to the urgings of former European colonies, and the United States followed suit in 1976. In 1979, as part of the Tokyo Round discussed in the previous section, the GSPs were given legal status within the GATT framework. The GSPs thus enabled GATT members to accord developing countries "preferential treatment for imports of specified goods."[40]

In essence, the GSP formula was a first step in the direction of diffuse reciprocity. Rather than seeking equivalent exchange, the industrial countries were now prepared to extend preferential treatment to LDCs on certain products. This decision can hardly be explained on a mercantilist basis. As Robert Hudec pointed out many years ago, it reflected an understanding by international trade negotiators that they had to "sacrifice for the common good."[41]

This should not lead us to exaggerate the moral value added of the GSP. The new regime still permitted industrial countries to maintain high import barriers. Further, it did not require *any* liberalization on the part of developing countries, and thus, more appropriately, exemplified unilateral as opposed to diffuse reciprocity. As a consequence, developing countries themselves were—and remain—slow to liberalize their internal markets, with negative consequences for their development and growth.

Indeed, GSPs, along with the "special and differential" status (S&D) that developing countries were accorded in subsequent trade negotiations (which has relieved them of the demands of specific reciprocity) would ultimately be challenged by many of the parties concerned, like affirmative action in the context of American domestic policies. Ideological opponents of the S&D principle, as well as a growing number of developing countries themselves, came to question whether preferential treatment really advanced the cause of freer trade and economic growth.

Again, many of the problems associated with this preferential treatment have resulted from *domestic* political economy. Because the international community did not place much pressure on developing countries to open their markets in reciprocal fashion, they simply did not do so, and therefore did not benefit from the domestic gains to trade. Whether the society of states *should* have placed more pressure on them is another question. My own view is yes, in the name of *diffuse* reciprocity, which places obligations on *both* parties. Still, it is notable that the trade regime has recognized something like a Rawlsian "difference principle" among nations, and although the role of S&D status as an engine of trade promotion is very much in dispute, it remains a necessary component of a fair trade regime.

Distributive Justice and Intellectual Property Rights

Although it is not my purpose in this book to discuss in any detail the present-day trade regime or current policy disputes over market access, certain moral questions of justice have risen so high on the international agenda in recent years that they usefully highlight some of the arguments presented here. Among these questions, few are as prominent and emotional as the question of trade-related intellectual property rights (TRIPS), especially when it comes to patented medicines. This is, quite literally, a matter of life and death, and one that our theory of justice *should* speak to in a way that clarifies the debate.

The issue of access to First World drugs by developing countries, especially access to therapies that can help in the fight against AIDS, has become a classic case of justice in the global economy. In the late 1990s, this dispute entered the world stage in the form of a legal conflict. It has lingered long since as a moral one.

In 1997, the South African government signed into law a new Medicines Act that granted the minister of health "the power to authorize parallel imports and compulsory licenses" of patented drugs, including AIDS antiretroviral therapies (parallel imports of drugs means in this context imports of generic substitutes from countries, such as India, that traditionally have not awarded property rights protection to pharmaceutical manufacturers in the form of patents, enabling local firms to produce substitutes, which was not an international legal issue so long as these were produced solely for domestic consumption; compulsory licensing means ordering local pharmaceutical companies to manufacture generics, again overriding any patent protection that might exist).[42] In turn, the South African government was sued by the Pharmaceutical Manufacturers Association of South Africa (a trade group representing the major multinational drug companies), which challenged the Medicines Act as a violation of South Africa's commitment to intellectual property rights under the recently signed WTO TRIPS agreement. (Initially, this lawsuit won a sympathetic ear from the United States government, whose trade representative counseled South Africa to respect TRIPS disciplines, but under domestic political pressure the American position collapsed.)

TRIPS had been agreed to by the WTO member states as part of the Uruguay Round trade negotiations, and it included acceptance by the signatories of protection of pharmaceutical patents. The problem that motivated it was assertions by multinational enterprises that their technologies were being infringed on, a situation made worse by the ease of access to new technology that globalization made possible. These firms, including the pharmaceutical manufacturers, managed to make TRIPS a high priority of American trade negotiators.

The pharmaceutical lawsuit against South Africa did not so much prove a test case for TRIPS disciplines as it provided AIDS activists and a number of leading nongovernmental organizations (NGOs) with a unique opportunity for placing their ethical concerns on the international health agenda. After all, the plaintiffs were a group that included some of the largest and most profitable corporations in the world, which sold their AIDS therapies for many thousands of dollars per treatment per year, while the defendant, the South African government, presided over a poor country that was at the very epicenter of the AIDS catastrophe.

The cruel facts of AIDS are now widely known. In 2001, more than twenty-eight million inhabitants of sub-Saharan Africa were infected with HIV, meaning that "about 9 percent of all sub-Saharan inhabitants between the ages of 15 and 49 were HIV carriers." AIDS-related mortality in the region was more than two million in that year alone, "suggesting that the disease accounted for every fifth death." Over the previous decade, "perhaps 20 million sub-Saharan people have perished in the pandemic."[43] The global spread of this disease has made it a central preoccupation of public health officials in both industrial and developing world governments, even if the latter have little capacity for dealing with the problem.

The AIDS activists and NGOs, which included Oxfam and the French group Doctors without Borders (Médecins sans Frontières), sought an immediate withdrawal of the drug manufacturers' lawsuit, a weakening of the TRIPS regime as it applied to pharmaceuticals and public health—so that countries could import generic drugs or order compulsory licensing without legal threat—and an immediate reduction of the price of AIDS drugs that pharmaceutical companies charged in LDCs. Under this pressure, and given significant media attention, the lawsuit was eventually withdrawn, and a modification of the

TRIPS regime to meet public health emergencies was agreed to by WTO member states during the millenium Doha Development Round of trade negotiations.[44] At the same time, a number of drug companies have offered to donate AIDS therapies to developing countries or to sell them "at cost."

The controversy over whether poor countries should be obliged to respect TRIPS disciplines in the face of the AIDS emergency has brought pressing questions of international economic justice to the front page of major newspapers around the world. Why is the TRIPS agreement part of the trade regime in the first place, and is it fair to developing countries?[45] How should the responsibility for responding to the AIDS pandemic be distributed among the various actors who are involved? Do multinational pharmaceutical manufacturers have a moral obligation to provide their drug therapies free of charge or at low cost to developing countries? Do African governments have a responsibility to create health insurance schemes and to augment their public health budgets? Do the rich industrial states have an obligation to increase their foreign aid spending in the face of the AIDS catastrophe? Where is the site of distributive justice in meeting a global challenge of this kind?

A useful starting point for addressing these questions is provided by the models of economic justice presented earlier in this book: the communitarian, cosmopolitan/prioritarian, and liberal internationalist frameworks. Under a communitarian or national welfare model of economic justice, governments have primary responsibility for the well-being of their citizens. The social pact within a given society reflects the distribution of obligations between a government and its people. In many societies, that social pact encompasses risk-sharing, so that some form of national health insurance (alongside social security, unemployment compensation, and other social policies) is provided to every individual. Normally, social programs of this kind are paid for in a progressive fashion, meaning that progressive taxation, for example, yields at least some of the financing for the communal scheme.

In many of the developing countries where the AIDS pandemic has reached its terrible heights, medical insurance schemes of this type are sorely lacking. The South African government, for example, has failed to put into place social insurance for its people. The problem is found not a priori in an absolute lack of funds, but in a domestic failure to redistribute funds from rich to poor. Throughout the developing world, governments have failed to introduce tax and budgetary schemes that are viewed as fair, and instead the wealthy often evade taxes and engage in capital flight, eroding the fiscal base. The point is that under the national welfare or communitarian framework, it is the responsibility of domestic societies to care for their sick and dying, in the way they see fit. Accordingly, societies have developed very different approaches to health care, from the National Health Service in Britain, which rations care on the basis of illness, age, and so forth (but not income)—maintained even under the government of Margaret Thatcher—to the more privatized system found in the United States, where the wealthy generally have access to higher levels of treatment.

I have already mentioned some of the limitations of the communitarian model in the first chapter, but here some more specific points can be made. First, many developing countries simply lack the administrative and medical capacity to deal with an epidemic of the magnitude presented by AIDS. Indeed, some would agree that the industrial world must accept its share of moral responsibility for that lack of capacity, to the extent that doctors, nurses, and others with skills are often greeted with open arms by—if not actively encouraged to migrate to—the United States, Western Europe, and other regions seeking these medical and scientific talents.

Second, AIDS is a global pandemic, limiting the effectiveness of national solutions. Clearly, if the AIDS crisis is to be overcome, it will only be on the basis of international cooperation in medical research and in treatment; more on this later in this section when I discuss the liberal internationalist approach.

Third, and related to the first two points, AIDS may not be a priority for national governments in the way it is for other members of the international community. This may be because AIDS victims—among whom one finds drug addicts, prostitutes, homosexuals, and others with little political voice—are shunned by their local societies, or because governments in developing countries may simply have other pressing priorities. But again, given its global nature, foreign nations may believe that they have a duty to intervene in the AIDS crisis if only to protect their own citizens against the disease.

This critique leads directly to the cosmopolitan or prioritarian view, which argues that each of us has a moral obligation to do what we can for those who are most vulnerable, no matter where they live. Since political boundaries are not ethical frontiers, those who suffer from AIDS in Africa or Asia should be treated no differently from our neighbors in rich countries who have this disease. It is only because of the accident of birth that those who are ill in rich countries have access to health insurance schemes and advanced medical technology, including drugs, modern hospitals, and specialized doctors and nurses. To the cosmopolitan theorist or activist, all of us who are capable of doing so should help the victims of AIDS around the world, even if those who are sick and dying live in societies that are poor, corrupt, or simply incapable of meeting the problem at hand.

Under the cosmopolitan view, the multinational pharmaceutical companies must also do what they can to assist those with AIDS. Very simply, this perspective "establishes a moral imperative to act." If one can "reduce great amounts of human suffering and thereby bring much 'happiness' to the world," then one should do it, whether as an individual or as a corporation.[46] The recent decisions by drug companies to reduce their anti-retroviral prices to developing countries or to donate them outright would be seen, from a cosmopolitan perspective, an appropriate response to the problem at hand. At the same time, prioritarians would probably support the right of governments to use parallel imports and compulsory licensing to get cheap drugs to patients, even if it meant infringing on international patents.

Yet there are problems with this perspective as well, even in the life-and-death case of AIDS. First, even if the members of the international community agreed that AIDS victims should be treated no matter where they are located, it does not follow they could agree on the priorities for such treatment. Should the international community aim its scarce resources at providing expensive anti-retrovirals to those already infected, or at preventing the disease when it comes to those at highest risk, such as truck drivers, drug users, and prostitutes, for example by more aggressive marketing of condoms and other safety measures? Answering these questions is hardly a straight-forward exercise, and they remain contested to this day. Indeed, the response will probably depend heavily on particular national circumstances.

Second, even if the members of the international community agreed that AIDS victims should be treated, it does not follow that they could agree on who should pay for the treatment. Is it the responsibility of the industrial world to increase foreign assistance flows to pay for drugs, or is it the responsibility of the pharmaceutical companies to donate their patented medicines? Again, answering these questions is hardly a straightforward exercise. For example, placing pressure on firms to donate drugs may reduce their incentives to invest in AIDS-related pharmaceutical research.

Finally, even if the members of the international community agree that AIDS victims should be treated, no matter where they are found, it does not follow that the target countries of this largesse would accept that AIDS programs are the highest priority for foreign intervention. This raises the question: who decides what developing countries "need" from foreign donors? And that question leads to our next perspective.

The liberal internationalist would adopt a middle ground with respect to this particular case. From this viewpoint, the members of the society of states should seek to reach agreements that are of mutual advantage, not only in the hope of producing public goods such as better health, but also in the interest of avoiding public "bads" such as the global spread of epidemics. The society of states should confront the AIDS problem and others like it on the basis of diffuse reciprocity, with each member contributing resources in order to help the poorest states meet the health challenges they face. Such a policy is both moral *and* self-interested.

It must be stressed that the concept of diffuse reciprocity that is fundamental to our conception of international distributive justice also places obligations on the recipient countries to fulfill their responsibilities. Cosmopolitan theorists sometimes fail to take seriously enough this issue of *governmental responsibility*. Unfortunately, foreign aid programs are not likely to be very effective so long as local governments are unwilling or unable to create sound domestic policy frameworks.

In the specific case at hand, the necessary policies include the establishment of public health programs and social insurance schemes. Should funds for combating AIDS simply fuel the fire of corruption, or should governments not want the funds in the first place, then support from the international community becomes much harder to justify. In the absence of governments that are willing to meet their basic responsibilities to their citizens, the cosmopolitan desire of helping those who are in need will inevitably be disappointed, despite all the good will in the world.

Yet it must also be emphasized that many developing-world governments have taken public health concerns— including the AIDS pandemic—seriously, and have made great strides in improving the health of their citizens, despite enormous challenges. A recent study highlights the role of developing-world governments in responding to a host of public health challenges, and it finds that "success is possible even in the poorest of countries."[47] When governments commit resources to fighting the diseases that ravage their populations, a just international community would stand ready to assist them in that effort with technical assistance and financial resources.

International Trade and National Welfare

In this chapter I have made the case that international trade must play a significant role in the development prospects of nations. But greater openness to trade may prove disruptive of the domestic social compact, as the factors of production get reallocated to more productive uses. In that process, some people will inevitably lose their jobs and their incomes, and the utilitarian response that they are contributing to the greater good is unlikely to move them. As Ravi Kanbur has written, "Rare is the development project, policy or process that only creates winners. . . . [D]isplacement is often part of the development footprint."[48] What should be done to compensate those who are on the losing end of economic change? In this section we begin to answer that question.

Liberal economists have long had trouble with the compensation principle that must be at the heart of domestic social arrangements for meeting the needs of those who are harmed by economic change. This debate is particularly heated in the field of international trade, perhaps because its distributive effects are predictable and, at least in theory, quite dramatic. As Harrison, Rutherford, and Tarr have written, "Trade policy reforms typically result in some households winning and some households losing. Given the diversity of households in an actual economy, even the most attractive reforms will typically result in some households losing. . . . One approach is just to accept these losses if they are 'acceptable,' as the price of achieving some greater good. Another approach is to argue against any reform that hurts even one household, especially if that household is poor."[49]

The first approach is utilitarian; the latter is Paretian or liberal. In seeking to reconcile the conflict between the increased wealth that freer trade would bring society as a whole, coupled with the losses or reduced welfare it would bring to certain groups, John Stuart Mill posited the "compensation principle" in the mid-nineteenth century. As Douglas Irwin describes Mill's principle, "if compensation is paid to those whose incomes fall under free trade, no one would be worse off and everyone could potentially be better off. In this case, free trade would prove best not just for national wealth, but for national welfare as well."[50] That insight would prove especially valuable to the founder of modern welfare economics, Vilifredo Pareto.

Rejecting utilitarian logic, Pareto argued, as a good liberal, that a policy change could only be justified when someone was made better off without anyone else becoming worse off, and he recognized that compensation would generally be necessary to achieve that result. But the Pareto principle has proved devilish to apply in practice, with few issues more challenging either theoretically or in terms of public policy than the design of appropriate compensation packages. This is certainly true in the case of free trade.

For example, although "just" compensation could be provided in theory in the form of lump-sum transfers that make up for, say, the income losses faced by displaced workers, the problem is that these transfers require a degree of information about households—their current and likely future income streams—that is very difficult to obtain (this is to say nothing of the incentives faced by displaced workers to misrepresent their likely future income streams in the hope of winning larger transfers). To be sure, many alternative forms of compensation have been proposed that do not rely on targeting of this sort, but each of them has been found wanting in some fundamental way. As a result, Brecher and Choudhri, among others, have asserted the "unfeasibility of Pareto gains from trade liberalization."[51]

Yet the view that displaced workers are owed compensation on equity grounds may be disputed. The reason is that, to the extent that workers in import-sensitive industries accrued a rent during the protectionist or pre–free trade era (that is, because they were protected by import barriers, their wages, or rents, were pushed to artificially high levels), they have no claim to compensation now that these barriers have been reduced or dismantled. In this sense, the earlier social compact, forged under protection, was unjust to particular societal groups.

Elaborating on this point, if our concern in justice is with those who are least advantaged or with the poor, it is unclear whether displaced workers would even fall into this category after trade opening. For we can expect free trade to help the poorest citizens by increasing their incomes through the lower prices they pay for consumer goods. Further, the economic growth that ensues may increase demand for their labor. If trade helps the poor in these ways, we may say that it is equity-enhancing.

Still, in the interest of fairness, societies that alter their economic policies and move toward greater openness will have obligations to those who are harmed by this policy change (in the next chapter, I will discuss the role of the international community in assisting developing countries in this respect). That does not make the issue of formulating compensation policies an easy one, but governments must respond to the challenge if they are to defend globalization as a policy that strengthens the domestic social compact. In this context it is notable that trade adjustment assistance and similar programs have been incorporated into nearly every postwar trade bill, at least in the United States and most of the other major industrial countries.

Conclusions

In this chapter, I have tried to provide a model of justice in trade. I have argued that, in theory, trade can be used as an instrument for creating an inclusive and participatory global economy, while enhancing the growth and welfare of each member state. At the same time, I have shown that the present-day trade regime is discriminatory in important respects, remaining tilted against developing countries.

In particular, I have cast doubt on the fairness of one of the key pillars of present-day international trade negotiations, namely the use of strict reciprocity. Although strict reciprocity has undoubtedly promoted the cause of trade liberalization between the United States and its European trading partners, it has failed to assist many developing countries that have sought market access, particularly in agriculture and textiles—sectors that remain heavily protected in the "North." Rather than promoting inclusion, strict reciprocity has effectively excluded many states from the trade deliberations. Accordingly, I have made the case that, in justice, states would instead negotiate on the basis of diffuse reciprocity, in which each country would have obligations and responsibilities, but with trade "concessions" being a function, say, of economic size.

Surprisingly, we have seen that considerations of justice and fairness have played a role in shaping trade agreements, if not in altering the basic structure of the trade regime itself. The outcomes of trade negotiations cannot be neatly explained solely by reference to either the mercantile interests of states or the economic desire to promote global efficiency. There is an important unexplained "residual," which we associate with the pursuit of justice or fairness. It appears that the parties have genuinely tried to reach agreements that each state could view as being fair, even if those agreements are nested within the context of an unjust international structure.

Over time, however, the unfairness of the trade regime has become increasingly palpable and demands for its revision increasingly widespread. That, for example, was the message delivered by the developing countries at the failed Cancun trade summit of September 2003—a trade summit that was allegedly devoted to development, but which could not deliver much by way of agricultural liberalization. Today, the agricultural policies of the United States and the European Union are in the spotlight, and their unfairness has become a source of embarrassment and international criticism. As political pressure mounts against these policies, we may expect reforms slowly to occur.

One issue that we will defer until later concerns some of the cross-border externalities commonly associated with free trade. Specifically, the interdependence of national economies implies that country S may engage in a set of labor practices that country N finds unfair or morally disturbing. Some observers of the international trading system have argued, for example, that "low" labor standards in developing countries create a "race to the bottom," which must inevitably hurt workers everywhere, undermining their wages and benefits. In chapter 4, I will explore the role of the international community in settling these sorts of disputes. Before doing so, however, I will discuss the other critical pillar of a just world economy beyond free trade, namely foreign assistance.

3

ALLOCATING AID

Poverty anywhere constitutes a danger
everywhere.
—Philadelphia Declaration of the
International Labor Organization, 1944

Only diehard protectionists would disagree with the proposition that trade plays an essential role in generating economic growth. More contested, however, is the notion that foreign aid can perform a similar function. To the contrary, aid is often viewed as growth-stifling to the extent that it fuels corruption, bloats the government, and creates disincentives for productive investment.

Why, then, should the international community assume, in the words of John Rawls, a "duty of assistance" in order to help states achieve their economic potential?[1] In what way can aid be considered welfare-enhancing, especially for donor countries? And even if a theoretical case for aid can be made, in practical terms how can aid be made effective? Across the political spectrum, these and other questions concerning the costs and benefits of foreign aid have been hotly contested.

Further normative questions arise with respect to *how* scarce foreign aid funds should be distributed among nations. Should they flow to the poorest states, or to the poorest persons? Should they be targeted exclusively at those states that have adopted "good" policies and institutions, or should they be disbursed with attention to regional balance?

It is these distributive questions that we take up in this chapter, since they go to the heart of contemporary normative debates that are actually shaping the allocation of scarce foreign aid funds in important respects. In order to see how normative theory helps influence decision rules with respect to aid allocation, consider the cosmopolitan/prioritarian and liberal internationalist approaches to that issue. For prioritarians, the main objective of aid is to assist the most vulnerable individuals, wherever they are located, by eliminating "global poverty" and ensuring the realization of some set of "basic human rights." Indeed, the leaders of the industrial world have pledged that "our goal is to eradicate poverty," and the United Nations has articulated an ambitious set of Millennium Development Goals (MDGs), which call for a substantial increase in aid funding, with that poverty-reduction objective in mind.[2] For liberal internationalists, in contrast, the primary goal of aid should be to provide poor or developing countries with the assistance they need to generate economic growth. The focus in this case is on helping states as opposed to helping any particular groups within the state.

In this chapter, we assess the strengths and weaknesses of a variety of aid allocation schemes in terms of our analysis that a just economic system is one that is inclusive, participatory, and welfare-enhancing for all—including for donor nations. We begin, however, with a brief review of why it is that states might concern themselves with providing foreign aid in the first place.

Foreign Aid and International Justice

Foreign aid has been a constant feature of the global economy since the end of World War II, if one whose effectiveness in promoting development has often been greeted with skepticism by policy analysts and elected officials.[3] The Marshall Plan notwithstanding, many observers—and the public at large—continue to believe that much foreign aid goes down the proverbial rat hole, fueling corrupt governments and simply round-tripping from bilateral and multilateral development agencies back to Swiss bank accounts. Although aid effectiveness is not my primary concern in this chapter, I recognize that many readers will be unconvinced by the claim that there can be justice in aid without a clearer demonstration that it makes a positive difference on the ground. That, however, is chiefly an empirical question, and readers who are so inclined can peruse that literature and draw their own conclusions. The widely accepted finding, however, is that aid that is targeted at public goods such as education, health care, and infrastructure plays a positive role in promoting growth and reducing poverty, especially in countries that have adopted "good" policies and institutions.[4]

A further critique of aid is that it is has always been a tool of power politics, used to curry favor with friends and allies, no matter how brutal the regime in question. The notion of "justice in aid" therefore has an oxymoronic quality. But that realist perspective has never illuminated the full story about the complex motivations behind foreign assistance.

It is David Lumsdaine who has most compellingly demonstrated that normative concerns have always played a role in shaping foreign aid policy, particularly in

Western Europe. "Support for aid" in these societies, he asserts, "was a response to world poverty which arose mainly from ethical and humane concern and, secondarily, from the belief that long-term peace and prosperity was possible only in a generous and just international order where all could prosper."[5] In this he echoed Gunnar Myrdal, who observed in his Nobel Prize address that after World War II, "The new awareness of poverty in underdeveloped countries was bound to be morally disturbing in the Western world where, particularly since the Enlightenment, the idea of greater equality has had an honored place in social philosophy."[6] Lumsdaine, like Myrdal, sought to show that foreign aid was an outward expression of the domestic social compact of European welfare states, and particularly the Scandinavian states with their strongly redistributive culture.

Today, a number of different normative arguments for foreign aid are still made by donors, ranging from the humanitarian to the realist, with each government adopting its own particular rationale for its largesse. But even after the argument for aid is made and accepted, the distribution of scarce aid funds remains a matter of debate. Should aid be focused on poor countries or poor persons? On consolidated democratic states, or countries with governance problems? How should aid be allocated to the developing world?

In the following sections, we will address these questions by examining several competing perspectives. First, I analyze the approach to foreign aid that is currently prominent in the World Bank and other aid agencies, which reflects the increasing influence of the cosmopolitan/prioritarian perspective. As we will see, this approach is problematic in important respects. I then examine

Rawls's duty of assistance, which focuses on aid as a means to support *political* development, also highlighting its difficulties. Notably, the aid policies of the United States under President George W. Bush have reflected this sort of philosophy. The president has established "Millennium Challenge Accounts," for which needy countries can only apply for aid if they "rule justly,"[7] and economists now uniformly argue that economic development depends on establishing "good governance," however defined. After that, I sketch my alternative theory, which elaborates on Roemer and Llavador's "equal opportunity" approach to aid, and argue that aid should be allocated in order to enable states to enter the international trading system. I conclude the chapter by discussing the critical role of foreign aid in maintaining the international trade regime through support for social safety nets in developing countries, as well as through balance-of-payments support.

Cosmopolitan Thought Meets Foreign Aid: International Welfare as Poverty Reduction

Many cosmopolitan thinkers, along with scholars and policy makers representing other theoretical orientations as well, would likely agree with the assertion that the top priority of the international aid community should be to end the scourge of poverty and its discontents—hunger, illiteracy, preventable disease—as quickly as possible. As already noted, the world's industrial leaders have pledged themselves to eradicate poverty and have established an ambitious set of Millennium Development Goals as targets. The rule of allocation or of distributive justice that follows from this principle is that aid dollars should be employed in order to achieve the maximum reduction in "global poverty." The specific policy issue facing aid bureaucrats under this cosmopolitan or prioritarian framework is how to get the greatest amount of poverty reduction from the smallest amount of aid, in other words, how to promote a "poverty-efficient" allocation of aid.

But that exercise is hardly straightforward. If our objective is to rid the world of poverty, do we simply transfer funds to the poorest people no matter where they live? Leaving aside the technical complications associated with such disbursements, are there no other distributive principles that we should consider in our allocation scheme, such as government type (and its responsibility for causing poverty and distress), or achieving a "fair" distribution of aid across countries? As we will see later, the cosmopolitan poverty-reduction scheme, with its emphasis on meeting the needs of the poorest individuals, is not so easy to put into practice.

According to two of the main proponents of the poverty-reduction approach to foreign assistance, Paul Collier and David Dollar, if we really "wish to maximize the reduction in poverty, aid should be allocated to countries that have large amounts of poverty and good [economic] policy."[8] Good policy, then, provides the basis for a secondary distributive criterion, alongside the presence of persons in poverty. This, of course, means that funds should *not* go, at least in the first instance, to persons who live in countries with "bad" policy, because this aid will not be very effective. But this reservation, of course, is problematic from a prioritarian standpoint.

Collier and Dollar's good policy variable is a composite drawn from the World Bank's country policy and institutional assessment (CPIA) scores, which cover some twenty different criteria including macroeconomic policy; microeconomic, structural, and trade policies; and public-sector management. To Collier and Dollar, foreign aid should flow solely to countries that have obtained relatively high CPIA scores; aid going to poor policy environments is unlikely, in their view, to be poverty-reducing. In some respects, this is supportive of the Rawlsian analysis, detailed later, that aid should be directed so as to support burdened societies with the establishment of decent or liberal institutions.

The reason for this focus on good policy, it must be stressed, is empirical rather than theoretical, and that is a point that needs to be emphasized and elaborated, for it is relevant to the other analytical frameworks that we will examine in the following sections. In order to illustrate the potential problems with this approach to justice in aid, let us imagine a hypothetical group of international negotiators who meet from behind a Rawlsian veil of ignorance—not knowing anything about their home countries—and are tasked with determining a just allocation of foreign assistance. It is doubtful whether they would commit to a decision rule based a priori on the existence of something called "good" policy, since they would probably have very different views about what good policy requires. During the early 1960s, for example, a wide variety of economies enjoyed strong growth, from the Soviet Union to Brazil to Sweden to the East Asian tigers. What these countries shared in terms of economic policy would have been difficult to discern; more on this later.

Yet another plausible policy that the negotiators might discuss is poverty reduction. That is, aid should be used to reduce poverty wherever it is found. But how is poverty most effectively reduced? Some might argue that it requires a drastic redistribution of resources from rich to poor, while others might argue for "trickle-down" theories. Given these various alternatives, it is unlikely that they could reach agreement on poverty reduction as the primary driver of aid allocations.

Rather than agree on a particular definition of "good policy" or adopt a focus on poverty reduction, our negotiators might therefore prefer to adopt some other decision rule, one that could be supported a priori, on a theoretical basis, as being crucial to the creation of an international economy that is inclusive, participatory, and welfare-enhancing, or based on the principle of mutual advantage. And I believe that the possibility for such a convergence of views is plausible. In a later section I will defend the allocative principle that aid should be used primarily to help states build the necessary capacity to enter the international trade regime.

In the event, being policy analysts rather than political theorists, Collier and Dollar's allocation scheme is an empirical one based on the causal connection they draw between good policy, economic growth, and poverty reduction; they therefore use a "three-step" approach to assessing aid allocations.[9] First, they estimate the impact of aid on growth. Second, they estimate the impact of growth on poverty reduction. Finally, they optimize the allocation of aid so that the maximum number of people is lifted out of poverty. Thus, aid goes to countries where it generates the most growth, which in turn brings the most people out of poverty. Because poverty-reducing economic growth is more likely to occur in countries with good policy, it is to these states that aid should flow. Using this framework in the present-day context, they find that "aid budgets would be allocated overwhelmingly to India.

Because India has reasonable policies, very high poverty, and a very large population, its capacity to absorb aid is enormous."[10]

But having drawn that conclusion, the authors then go on to dig themselves into a theoretical hole. Due to the fact that India would dominate foreign aid allocations in their model, the authors decide, for undisclosed reasons, to arbitrarily "constrain" or hold constant at present-day levels the amount of aid that Delhi would receive in their allocation model, focusing instead on a number of other country cases where additional foreign assistance should flow. These "high poverty/good policy" countries would include, for example, Uganda, Bangladesh, and Ethiopia. On the flip side, countries that would receive little or no aid would include (relatively) low poverty/good policy developing countries, such as Chile, not to mention the many high poverty/bad policy countries spread throughout the developing world, but concentrated mainly in sub-Saharan Africa.

Collier and Dollar's arbitrary shift of aid away from India toward other developing countries is puzzling, at least from the cosmopolitan perspective. For it suggests that another principle of distributive justice is at work that is never formally articulated. Is it geographic, meaning that aid should also be allocated "fairly" across regions? They do not explicitly tell us why they abandon the "pure," poverty-efficient model, in which the bulk of aid funds flow to one country, India. To be sure, it seems unlikely that a cosmopolitan theorist, much less an international bureaucrat, would wish to see the all world's scarce aid funds benefit the poor in India, no matter how deserving they might be. But how *would* they allocate aid?

It is also crucial to emphasize that the authors are skeptical about the value of "targeting" aid *directly* to the poor so as to raise their *relative* incomes; that is, they do not believe that aid can be used successfully to influence the domestic income distribution. As an empirical matter, they find that aid tends to have neutral consequences on the income distribution, meaning that it benefits all income groups in more or less equal measure. Because of the difficulty that foreign aid agencies have in influencing domestic income distributions (and one must question whether it would be just to seek to influence another country's domestic social compact along income lines), their model is predicated on a view that aid should be thought of as helping the poor in *absolute* (as opposed to relative) terms through the channels provided by economic growth.

Aid that supports a major infrastructure project, for example, may have neutral effects on the income distribution within a country, but it could help boost the poor's income in absolute terms. An example of this would be a new road that enables a small farmer to get his crops to market faster, reducing spoilage and the associated monetary loss in sales.

Many other criticisms can also be leveled at Collier and Dollar's quasi-prioritarian approach to foreign aid. First, as already noted, we may doubt the *theoretical* value of a distributive principle based on good policy, since there is no a priori agreement on what that means. Second, perhaps an argument can be made that poverty-reducing aid should be based on bad policy instead of on good policy. Collier and Dollar, for example, seem to dismiss the possibility that aid can be used as a "carrot" for getting governments to adopt "good" economic policies; for them, it should only reward countries that have already adopted the neo-liberal prescriptions and put them into place. But countries may have bad policies for many reasons—for example, a lack of skilled bureaucrats—and aid could be used to relieve these bottlenecks. As Hansen and Tarp suggest, "countries that are less fortunate in having good policies in place may need help badly to bring them on track."[11] Conversely, countries with good policy may not be those most in need of scarce aid resources, since they will likely benefit from private-sector investment.

Third, despite the results of their cross-country regression analysis, it may be the case that "good" policy is less important for growth than they claim. In the neo-classical models of economic growth, policy did not figure as a growth variable at all. That is not surprising, for if one observed the growth of nations during the period, say, 1950–1970, it is not obvious that any single policy prescription dominated the growth charts. As already noted, Communist states, European welfare states, Latin American protectionist regimes, and East Asian export-oriented economies all did reasonably well. In this diverse set of country cases, capital accumulation and technological change were the key drivers of growth. That being the case, perhaps a poverty-efficient approach to foreign aid would aim at these neoclassical economic variables, making capital and technology available to countries that otherwise lacked these resources.

The failure of the quasi-cosmopolitan approach to address these theoretical and empirical questions satisfactorily suggests the difficulties of using the poverty-efficient model as the basis for our theory of justice in aid, as compelling as the objective of reducing "world" or "global" poverty might be. In the next section, we examine a very different model, proposed by the late John Rawls. He emphasized political rather than economic factors in development, but we will see the limits of this position as well.

A Rawlsian Model: Foreign Aid and "Burdened Societies"

In *The Law of Peoples*, John Rawls proposed an entirely different approach to the "duty of assistance." There he argued that a limited duty of assistance existed on the part of liberal, well-ordered polities in order to promote just social institutions within "burdened societies." Rawls insisted that burdened societies should not be defined as "poor" countries on an economic basis alone, although he did not specify which countries he had in mind. For Rawls, "burdened societies, while they are not expansive or aggressive, lack the political and cultural traditions, the human capital and know-how, and often the managerial and technological resources to be well-ordered. The long-term goal of relatively well-ordered societies should be to bring burdened societies . . . into the Society of well-ordered Peoples."[12] The purpose of foreign aid should therefore be to help these states "realize and preserve just (or decent) institutions, and not simply to increase . . . the average level of wealth, or the wealth of any society or any particular class in society."[13]

It is significant that Rawls did not extend his famous "difference principle," the idea that just societies should maximize the life chances of those who are least advantaged, to the level of the international system. He provided three reasons why the difference principle was not applicable as a principle of justice among nations (or what he called "peoples"). First, the international system is distinct from domestic politics in that it is constituted by a diversity of societies each of which, even if they are all liberal and well ordered, will have its own distinctive approach to the problem of distributive justice. We have stressed this crucial point in making the case that a just global economy must be inclusive, participatory, and welfare-enhancing—a system of mutual advantage—for each nation-state that wishes to enjoy the fruits of openness. Second, although a lack of "primary goods" may compromise the life chances of an individual, there is no corollary at the level of a society or country as a whole. This is because of Rawls's claim that "there is no society anywhere in the world—except for marginal cases—with resources so scarce that they could not, were it reasonably and rationally organized and governed, become well-ordered. Historical examples seem to indicate that resource-poor countries may do very well (e.g., Japan), while resource-rich countries may have serious difficulties."[14] This leads to the third point, which is that societies fail to prosper economically not because of an absence of natural resources, but because of flawed political cultures. For Rawls, once "just" political and social institutions are established *within* all the members of the society of states (or of peoples, as he calls them), then the international duty of assistance loses its raison d'être; again, this is different from the domestic social compact, where there will be a continuing need to help those who are least advantaged for any number of reasons (e.g., changes in income, aging, or health).

What would be Rawls's decision rule for granting assistance to burdened societies under his theoretical scheme? Drawing on the work of Amartya Sen, Rawls focused particularly on the presence or absence of "human rights."

Governments that grant assistance to burdened societies will do so in order to promote basic human rights, especially equal liberties across the gender divide. Conversely, governments that seek to benefit from the "duty of assistance" will have expressed their desire to develop their political culture in a liberal direction.

But having provided us with this decision rule, Rawls went on to acknowledge, "there is no easy recipe for helping a burdened society to change its political culture," as the United States has been learning in Afghanistan and Iraq as these words are being written.[15] Still, Rawls believed that justice and self-interest met in international politics, meaning that liberal societies would wish to provide such assistance because "well-ordered" regimes "are not dangerous but peaceful and cooperative." [16] Rawls's approach to the duty of assistance therefore draws heavily on "democratic peace" theory, or the empirical (if contested) observation that democracies do not go to war with one another.

Drawing on that theory, we can see why one might wish to allocate aid in order to promote democratization, and indeed democracy and human rights are central to the foreign assistance programs of the United States and the European Union. If democracy is essential to peace and prosperity, then it would make good sense for the international community to allocate aid solely to nations with democratic institutions.

The promotion of democracy is not, however, central to the approach to justice in aid that I will adopt here, although I fully appreciate its normative (and perhaps even empirical) appeal. One reason is that the phrase *democratic peace theory* is something of a misnomer; as noted above, the democratic peace is an empirical regularity rather than a theoretical proposition (although Rawls asserted that because democracies are "satisfied" internally, they are not aggressive externally). We do not possess any robust theories of why democracies do not go to war with one another; that is simply a "fact," albeit one that has been disputed by some analysts, who argue that democratic peace theorists have conveniently defined democracy to meet their data.

Until we establish the theoretical basis for the democratic peace more firmly, and conversely establish arguments as to why authoritarian regimes are inherently less peaceful and welfare-oriented, it would be hard to justify democratization as our primary decision rule for allocating aid. Along these lines, however, one intriguing hypothesis for democratic peace theory is that it is the stability of democratic *institutions* that makes it more likely that interactions among democracies will be viewed by governments as iterated games, which promote the prospects for cooperation by ensuring future interactions. Under an authoritarian regime, in contrast, it is difficult to know what policy will look like after the leader dies or is overthrown. If it is indeed the case that structural characteristics *within* democracies lead to iterated economic relationships *among them*, then democratic peace theory would come to possess a theoretical basis that might give democracies—assuming that consolidated democracies can be established in developing countries—a stronger foundation for making claims on scarce aid resources. [17]

In the meantime, since there is no a priori reason why a nondemocratic state could not be equally peaceful, prosperous, and trustworthy as a democratic one—a reasonably enlightened but still authoritarian regime such as Singapore comes to mind—it is unclear why the society of states would exclude such countries from membership in international institutions or wish to deny them access to foreign aid should the need arise. Rawls himself admitted that, in any event, he possessed no theory of how to transform a burdened society into a liberal or well-ordered one, *and indeed no such theory exists*. In the absence of such a theoretical framework, therefore, it is difficult to use this approach as a building block for our model of justice in aid.

Liberal Internationalism and the "Equal Opportunity" Approach to Aid

Liberal internationalists would agree with Rawls in holding that economic justice must be built among the members of the society of states. A state system that is concerned with fairness would be one that is inclusive, participatory, and welfare-enhancing for all. But what are the implications of this line of analysis for the distribution of foreign aid? Let us consider some of the alternatives.

One approach might be to provide aid primarily to countries that are experiencing slow rates of growth. Since the conditional convergence hypothesis suggests that the potentially highest growth rates are to be found among countries that are farthest from their long-run growth path—that is, the greater the difference between $[y^* - y_i]$ (where y^* = the country's long-run per capita income, and y_i = its current per capita income)—then aid should flow to such countries. This sort of aid would be welfare-enhancing for all, including donor countries, to the extent that more rapid growth in poor countries would increase the size of the global economic pie. It will be noted that this model says nothing about good policy or poverty reduction; its sole emphasis is on growth rates.

This approach could prove attractive to our hypothetical international negotiators. It enables each country to pursue its own socioeconomic model while relying on the international system for the additional capital and technology needed to boost domestic growth rates. So long as the polity in question is not aggressive, then such an approach could be consistent with a theory of international economic justice based on mutual advantage among sovereign equals. In this spirit, David Miller asks, what would "global justice . . . require if there are states which simply cannot command the resources" to achieve sustained growth? The answer, he says, "is development aid of the traditional sort, that is, long-term investments by outside agencies and technology transfers to build up the resource base of the society."[18]

Yet our would-be negotiators might pause before striking an agreement in which aid transfers were based on low growth rates or on a lack of technological resources. One problem that would undoubtedly concern them is moral hazard. They might fear that the provision of aid to low-growth nations could provide the wrong signals to the target countries. The aid message could be interpreted to mean that poor performance is somehow being rewarded by the society of states. As a result, states will lack the motivation or incentive to increase their growth rates through appropriate domestic policy measures.

Accordingly, states might seek to attach some conditions to their assistance, and this brings us back to the discussion of good policy, with all the limitations noted earlier. In a brilliant piece that combines theories of justice with economic models and data, Humberto Llavador and John Roemer argue that a just allocation of aid would be one that promotes "equal opportunity" for growth among countries, rewarding states that exhibit what they call "effort" or what would more conventionally be labeled by mainstream economists as "good policy" (e.g., macroeconomic stabilization, trade openness, and so forth).[19]

Returning to the discussion of equal opportunity found in the first chapter, Llavador and Roemer suggest that economic growth may be viewed as a function of two broad variables: "circumstances," which would include initial income, ethnic fractionalization, and several institutional features of the society; and "effort," which amounts to good (macroeconomic and trade) policy. Basically, what they seek to do is compute growth equations for particular countries based on their particular circumstances. They then examine the influence of good policies. Good policies enable countries to grow faster than their circumstances would normally allow; in essence, countries with good policy are "overachievers." It is to these countries, according to Llavador and Roemer, that scarce foreign aid resources should be allocated. This would provide a powerful incentive to other nations to adopt good policies, and as a consequence aid would be distributed so that every country can do as well as it can, given its "circumstances."

It is important to emphasize that, unlike the cosmopolitan perspective discussed earlier, Llavador and Roemer *do not* seek to allocate aid for the purpose of poverty reduction among *persons*; instead, it is to promote the growth chances of each and every *country*. Indeed, Llavador and Roemer recognize that their model is quite different from the current aid allocation scheme carried out by bilateral lending agencies, which they claim "predominantly give aid to countries which are important with regard to their international economic and military interests." They are hopeful, however, that "considerations of justice are . . . more prominent in the decisions of multilateral agencies."[20] As we have seen, that is probably the case, although the cosmopolitan model of justice that is apparently guiding that work remains problematic, and it is certainly not an "equal-opportunity" model, at least as sketched by Llavador and Roemer.

Under the Llavador-Roemer framework, aid allocations would quite explicitly be offered as a carrot for sound economic management. Most provocatively, perhaps, their equal-opportunity approach would provide less aid to poor African countries than is presently the case, since in their view most African governments have failed to implement good policies. Asian economies, in contrast, would receive relatively more aid than they have enjoyed up to now.

Yet from our perspective of building a *theory* of international economic justice, the use of "good" policy as the basis for aid allocations is still problematic. However, there is at least one economic policy on which our hypothetical negotiators could agree, and that is greater openness to trade and investment—policies that are of mutual advantage for all. A just allocation of aid, therefore, would be one that assists economies as they seek to enter the global economy by exercising their comparative advantage. Such an allocation would meet our principles of international economic justice: that the global economy be inclusive, participatory, and welfare-enhancing for each and every state.

What does this mean precisely? It means that countries would focus their aid on helping states that require assistance to build up their trade-related infrastructure along with their trade capacity frameworks and institutions. Particularly, many developing nations require increased analytical capacity in order to negotiate agreements with the great economic powers, which have ready access to teams of economists and lawyers. Further, aid could be used to help the economic "losers" produced by the move to free trade, by providing them with education, training, and social safety nets. After all, the implementation of free trade agreements may "demand much from the institutional and human capacities of poor countries" (more on this in the next section).[21] It could require the adoption of new domestic regulations and health and safety standards. A country that opens itself to food and drug imports, for example, will wish to ensure that these products are safe, and even if it relies on the exporting nation for such information it will need local capacity to ensure that the information that has been provided is reliable. We must not forget that it is ultimately domestic governments that are responsible for the welfare of their people.

Scholars and policy makers often overlook the requirement for trade capacity building, but it is hardly trivial if we seek to construct a just global economy, or one that is of mutual advantage to all states. After all, it is one thing to sign a trade agreement, another to have the wherewithal to enjoy its benefits. Helping countries enter the trading system should therefore be the primary objective of foreign aid. Such an aid policy would not only be coherent, but it would also serve the greater cause of economic justice.

At present, we know that this is not the case, and that the barriers to entry for global economic transactions are high; after all, most international trade is dominated by multinational corporations that effectively shape trade patterns, and are armed with experts to help steer them through the murky waters of trade legislation. As Richard Blackhurst and his associates have written of sub-Saharan Africa, several "incapacities" impede states from entering the trading system, including "inadequate capacity for monitoring and analysing the trade policies of key trading partners and limited supply of qualified personnel with requisite knowledge of matters of international trade law." In some countries, there is "near total ignorance of the functioning of the multilateral trading system and lack of technical expertise."[22]

Given these shortfalls, Blackhurst and his colleagues have called on "donors . . . to increase their support and assistance to well-coordinated programs of institutional development that enhance the capacity of developing countries . . . to participate effectively in the international trading system, and to permit them to meet their obligations in the WTO. Such institutional strengthening is a *sine qua non* for effective representation of African countries' interests in the WTO, as well as for the accession to the WTO of countries which are not yet members."[23]

Foreign assistance for capacity building will therefore be of critical importance to developing countries that seek to participate in the international trading system. Gaining information on export markets and the various nontariff barriers to trade could prove costly and time-consuming to the entrepreneurs and government officials in developing countries. In these states, where the private sector is likely to be made up mainly of small and medium-sized enterprises, the international economy poses major "barriers to entry," and globalization may appear as a tidal wave that overwhelms societies, rather than as a tide that lifts all boats. These barriers to market access could be seen as unfair and assistance in overcoming them is consistent with our theory of justice as equal opportunity.

Yet another task of capacity building is to ensure that trade negotiators are able to work effectively within the multilateral context. Even a truly free trade regime would raise thorny analytical issues for national policy makers. How will openness influence domestic labor and product markets, and environmental policies? These sorts of issues can be answered only by using sophisticated tools and techniques, which may be costly for developing countries to procure. Providing assistance toward that end would provide a boon to the free-trade agenda and, in turn, to the cause of international economic justice.

It should also be emphasized that this approach to foreign assistance may also be conceived of as being "pro-poor," in that increases in trade are positively associated with absolute income gains for the bottom income deciles, partly because trade often leads to lower prices. But this approach does not claim to solve the problem of income distribution *within* societies, which must be a topic for the domestic social compact. The best that the society of states can do is to create circumstances in which each country can do as well as it can. By opening the door to free trade through support for infrastructure and capacity building, and by helping states in difficulty maintain their commitment to open markets with limited financial support, the international community is fulfilling its duty of assistance.

Foreign Aid, Domestic Crises, and International Stability

The move to greater openness may prove disruptive to the domestic social compacts of developing countries no less than those of industrial countries. The "shock" of openness could create frictional unemployment and increase the demand for education and training, and for social safety nets. Without these policies in place, the disruptions caused by economic change could threaten domestic stability. A just international system will help states to finance social safety nets and other compensatory policies in the interest of welfare-enhancing peace and prosperity. As Rodrik has written, social insurance "cushions the blow of liberalization among those most severely affected, it helps maintain the legitimacy of these reforms, and it averts backlashes against the distributional and social consequences of integration into the world economy."[24]

It has sometimes been argued by economists that a larger welfare state is necessarily associated with increasing economic interdependence. The underlying hypothesis here is that as countries open themselves to the world economy, their industries and workers face terms-of-trade risks against which only governments can provide insurance. This is particularly the case for small economies. Confronted by increasing economic volatility, the workforce demands social safety nets as the price for a more open trade policy. Supporting these theoretical arguments is the empirical finding that open economies tend to have bigger governments.[25]

To be sure, the challenges facing developing countries in the implementation of social policy are many and appear almost overwhelming. Beyond the fiscal weaknesses that most of these countries face, including widespread tax avoidance and capital flight, severe administrative limitations must also be confronted. Further, the advancement of certain policies, including pension reform and unemployment compensation, requires the creation of entirely new institutions, such as independent regulatory bodies, that in turn rely on other institutions, such as the rule of law, which may be very weak. In short, throughout the developing world, social policies must be introduced in the context of limited state capacity, on the one hand, and rapidly rising demand for social insurance and assistance, on the other.

Given these domestic administrative and political-economy difficulties, it is not surprising to find external assistance playing such a large role in the funding and reform of social safety net programs in the developing world. According to a study prepared by the United Nations, bilateral and multilateral aid programs in Africa and Latin America have borne a large share of domestic social-sector costs. The World Bank, the International Monetary Fund, the European Union, and other donors have also contributed significantly in both financial and intellectual terms to social policy reform in the post-Communist transition economies.[26]

The relationship between the global economy and domestic social disruption has critical implications for foreign aid beyond the financing of social safety nets. Of greatest significance, it means the provision of balance-of-payments support, in order to help countries maintain open markets at times when economic conditions unleash strong protectionist pressures. *Indeed, bringing these two policies together—balance-of-payments support and social safety nets—is essential for building a system of international economic justice.* In the nineteenth century, a Russian foreign minister lamented, "we export even though we die." In a just international system, no trade or finance minister would wish to hear these words from a colleague.

The reason why balance-of-payments support is so essential to a stable global economy is because without it, states will be tempted to adopt protectionist policies during periods of recession, in order to maintain full employment in support of the domestic social contract. There is thus a potential tension between free trade and full employment—between the domestic and international social compacts. That tension could rip international cooperation to shreds.

It is no coincidence that many of the multilateral economic institutions that dominate today's landscape, such as the International Monetary Fund and the World Bank, were first established in the wake of the Great Depression and World War II, for these crises exemplified the inability of the members of the society of states to resolve their domestic economic problems in a peaceful manner. Incapable of a cooperative response to the Great Depression, the society of states allowed the economic tensions being produced within each member to spill over into the international system as a whole, helping to spark the flames of war. Avoiding this possibility will be one of the major preoccupations of the society of states, and it highlights the difference between a world in which mercantilist interests rule the roost versus one in which norms of fairness, inclusion, and participation inform policymaking. Again, we see that such norms can promote the robustness and stability of the international system and world economy.

To be specific, let us suppose that a developing world economy has to import food in order to nourish itself. All other things being equal, a rise in world food prices would result in lower consumption and perhaps increased hunger. A just international system will provide that country with balance-of-payments support in order to continue its food purchases, while necessary economic adjustments are made in order to reduce the human suffering associated with higher prices. Without such aid, social disruption could occur that spills over into the international system.

In a similar vein, countries faced with domestic economic difficulties may be tempted to "export" those problems overseas, perhaps through the implementation of competitive currency devaluations. Such devaluations could lead to a "beggar-thy-neighbor" situation in which international exchange quickly becomes endangered. Again, a just system will seek to avoid that temptation by providing states with balance-of-payments and foreign exchange support in order to smooth any adjustments that must be made.

In short, a just international system will enable states to enjoy the benefits both of free trade and of full employment. The critical link between the two is found in international financial support. Something like an "International Monetary Fund" would therefore play a key institutional role in a just global economy, for it would provide the balance-of-payments financing that helps keep markets open at a time when pressures to close them are at their highest point. Looked at from this angle, it is indeed ironic that the International Monetary Fund has been the target of antiglobalization activists, for that institution, as much as any other, is the very linchpin that holds together the domestic and international economies.

Without such an institution, the threat of a decisive split between the two, with devastating results for the world's global prosperity, would be all the greater.

Conclusions

Foreign aid will play a central role in building a just global economy. But how should we allocate this aid? As we have seen, there are many answers to that question. In this chapter, I have defended the idea that aid should be used to assist countries that are seeking to exercise their comparative advantage and enter the global trading system, by focusing on infrastructure support, capacity building, the knitting of social safety nets, and balance-of-payments support.

To be sure, this framework, like the others discussed here, requires further elaboration. Each model of justice in aid has significant theoretical and empirical limitations that need to be addressed in greater detail. But clarifying the greater purpose of foreign aid in contributing to international prosperity, and assessing the underlying principles and assumptions behind different distributive schemes, can help bring greater rigor to these public discussions. In this way, political theory can contribute directly to contemporary policymaking, and, we would hope, to furthering the cause of international economic justice.

Readers will be painfully aware that I have not mentioned in this chapter the contentious issue of aid *effectiveness*. As a theoretical proposition, I have made the case for aid and simply assumed that such assistance is effective. That requires a leap of faith, since aid effectiveness has been seriously questioned by any number of critics, just as the costs and benefits of welfare spending have been constantly questioned within advanced industrial societies. These debates over effectiveness, of what works and what does not, are likely to become more heated in the years ahead as the case for greatly increasing foreign aid to meet the Millennium Development Goal of eradicating world poverty is made by scholars, activists, and many policy makers. Still, if moral theory can address the larger purpose of aid, and of how such aid should be targeted, its contribution to that debate will have been largely fulfilled.

4

JUSTICE IN MIGRATION
AND LABOR

The first essential is to accept that the voters'
right to a say about who and how many can enter
must take precedence over the rights of those
unlucky enough to be born in poorer parts
of the world.
—*The Economist*, 2002

A just global economy is necessarily built atop two social compacts: one *among* nation-states, and another *within* them. The first compact offers the promise of greater economic growth via the pathway of international trade and investment, while the second, domestic social compact signifies an agreement between government and society to exploit that growth in the interest of producing greater welfare for the polity as a whole.

But what if, rather than strengthening the domestic social compact, greater openness to trade and investment acts to *undermine* it? For example, suppose that states of type N with relatively high labor standards (e.g., health and safety standards, minimum wages, and the right to association) believe that their import-sensitive industries are losing their competitive edge and market share to firms in countries of type S with much lower labor standards. How should N respond? Would it be just to employ tariffs or sanctions aimed at coercing higher labor standards in S? What is the appropriate role of the international community in resolving conflicts of this type? These are among the issues I address in this chapter.

Many of the alleged injustices found in today's labor markets could, in theory, be mitigated by freer migration flows of workers from poor to rich countries. That, in a sense, was the nineteenth century's solution to the problem of low labor standards. In the absence of welfare states that provided workers with unemployment compensation and social safety nets during economic hard times, Europe's surplus labor sought new opportunities and higher wages in the United States, South America, and Australia. If there is one major difference between globalization today and a century earlier, it is in our much more restrictive treatment of migration.

But there are many normative questions associated with labor migration that provide significant challenges for a theory of economic justice, bringing contending theoretical perspectives into especially sharp relief. What would justice in migration consist of? Would it be "free," like trade in goods and services? How can migration be made to work on behalf of source as well as destination countries? In other words, is it possible to think of migration as a system of mutual advantage?

In this chapter, I use the issues of migration and labor standards as a way of addressing the broader topic of the conflicts in *values* that must inevitably arise among the members of an interdependent economic system, each having its own domestic social compact. To be sure, many of the contemporary economic disputes among states, over things such as cultural preferences, genetically modified organisms, migration, and labor and environmental standards, are really about the pressures placed on governments by their special interest groups, which can be resolved, at least in theory, in pecuniary fashion through mechanisms such as side payments.

But not all the debates among states are material in nature. They are also shaped by the different sets of values that continue to distinguish and to divide "autonomous" societies. In this context, consider the example of France and the United States, two highly globalized industrial societies, with very different approaches to a wide variety of political and economic issues. In France, many people seem to believe that it is consistent to decry the importation of genetically modified crops for health reasons, on the one hand, while continuing to smoke with reckless abandon, on the other. In the United States, smoking is now largely prohibited in public spaces, but many Americans are eating themselves to obesity. In France, nuclear power is generally accepted as a safe and reliable source of energy, while in the United States it is nearly impossible for an electric utility to build a nuclear power plant. These differing risk profiles are not simply about economics and cost-benefit calculations, although pecuniary interests are surely present; they are also about societal values that are much harder to quantify.[1] It must therefore come as no surprise that states may clash when their differing values meet in the global economy; how to resolve them in justice is a difficult question. This issue of differing values leads us to ask: Under what circumstances should the members of society A be legitimately concerned with the social compact in society B, and attempt to intervene in its structure?

In this chapter, I will seek to explore these questions as follows. First, I examine the issue of justice in migration, contrasting the communitarian and cosmopolitan approaches to this topic before providing a liberal internationalist perspective, which emphasizes the possibility of migration as a system of mutual advantage. I then turn to the problem of labor standards, and see whether an argument can be made for imposing a global set of labor standards on each and every country.

Justice in Migration: Rights or Welfare?

Few topics are more charged from the perspective of international justice than the migration of persons across borders.[2] How should we think about migration in ethical terms? Do we emphasize the *rights* of migrants versus those of citizens, or should we focus on migration's economic (among other) *consequences* for the concerned states and persons?[3] As John Roemer has pointed out, although most contemporary discussions of justice in migration tend to be framed in terms of human rights— specifically, the rights of people to migrate versus the rights of people, joined together in "self-sufficient" communities, to exclude—other approaches are helpful in illuminating this particularly thorny issue of international justice.[4]

In most renderings, the rights-based approach pits communitarian or national welfare theorists against cosmopolitans; that is, it pits those who believe that political associations such as states possess ethical borders against those who give precedence to the rights of individuals.[5] But each of these perspectives has important analytical limitations for a theory of international justice. As I will discuss later, the cosmopolitan position is problematic in important respects, for it assumes that emigrating individuals necessarily have equal or even greater rights than individuals in the destination country whose preference might be exclusion; and if we assume that the excluder has property rights, it is not obvious a priori why his rights would not be at least equal to if not greater than those of the migrant (unless we wish to assume some form of prioritarian condition on behalf of the migrant, in which we assert that this individual has, by force of his or her objective circumstances, rights that *override* those of the homesteader).

On the other hand, the communitarian perspective can be ostrich-like, overlooking the interest that the international community might take in a host of migration-related issues. Developing countries, for example, could be concerned by the "brain drain" and worker remittance flows, and these sorts of issues may be resolved to mutual advantage only on a bilateral or multilateral basis. More broadly, the members of the society of states might eventually come to agree that some minimal rights for migrants should be respected, so that individuals who are not full citizens of their countries of residence do not fall prey to exploitation.

This tension between human and sovereign rights was well put by the late Myron Weiner when he stated, "Underlying much of the debate over migration and refugee policies is the fundamental moral contradiction between the notion that *emigration* is widely regarded as a matter of human rights while *immigration* is regarded as a matter of national sovereignty" (italics added).[6] Compelling philosophical arguments on behalf of both the cosmopolitan and national welfare frameworks have been put forward with respect to migration policy. As Roemer summarizes the positions, "one can argue that the place of one's birth is a morally arbitrary matter, and equality of opportunity requires allowing each person to choose where to live. On the other hand, it can be argued that a nation creates a political culture (or a political community) whose reproduction depends upon maintaining a certain degree of homogeneity, and that the value of public culture endows citizens with the right to exclude others to that degree necessary for its maintenance."[7]

Beyond this focus on human rights, and perhaps even more useful for understanding the vast majority of migration flows in the world economy, one can also examine the motivations for—and consequences of—migration through the lens of social welfare or economic well-being, at the individual, national, and international levels. The studies produced to date that aim to model migration patterns from this perspective suggest that it holds great promise as the basis for a progressive research agenda.[8]

Further, nonutilitarians can also profitably make use of this work, perhaps refining their models as a result. John Rawls, for example, asserted in *The Law of Peoples* that migration was mainly a consequence of failed states and oppressive regimes. He wrote:

> There are numerous causes of immigration. I mention several and suggest that they would disappear in the Society of liberal and decent Peoples. One is the persecution of religious and ethnic minorities, the denial of their human rights. Another is political oppression of various forms. . . . Often people are simply fleeing from starvation. . . . Yet famines are often themselves in large part caused by political failures and the absence of decent government. The last cause I mention is population pressure in the home

territory, and among its complex of causes is the inequality and subjection of women. . . . Thus, religious freedom and liberty of conscience, political freedom and constitutional liberties, and equal justice for women are fundamental aspects of sound social policy for a realistic utopia. *The problem of immigration . . . is eliminated as a serious problem in a realist utopia.* [italics added][9]

In fact, Rawls's explanation covers only a fraction of global labor flows, and it is usefully supplemented by an economic framework. As Albert Berry and Ronald Soligo have pointed out in a pioneering paper, "the welfare implications" of international migration "have received very little theoretical treatment."[10] Because that is the case, it is useful to spend a moment thinking about the economic implications of, and motivations for, migration for both the sending and receiving countries, and for the individuals within them who either seek to migrate or who wish to restrict these flows. Building on this base, we can then return to the cosmopolitan, communitarian, and liberal internationalist approaches to justice in migration.

So let us begin by assuming that an individual's decision to migrate is driven solely by base economic motives. In the simplest possible model, migration is a function of wage differentials, such that

$$E = w_{fi} - w_{hi} - c > 0$$

where E is the decision to emigrate, w_{fi} are the wages in the destination country, and w_{hi} are wages in the home country; c is the cost of migration. It is worth emphasizing that this simple model suggests that the *motivation* to migrate may therefore remain strong even in an international society composed solely of liberal or "well-ordered"

TABLE 4.1
Immigration to the United States, 1991–1998

Immigrants from all countries: 7,338,062
U.S. population, 1995: 263,044,000
Immigrants as a percentage of U.S. population: 2.9
Immigrants from:

Europe	1,132,002
Asia	2,346,751
Americas	3,777,281
Africa	280,230
Oceania	45,584

Source: Andrés Solimano, "International Migration and the Global Economic Order" (World Bank Policy Research Working Paper 2720, November 2001), p. 30.

states. In this context, it is notable, for example, that between 1991 and 1998, more than one million Europeans migrated to the United States, including nearly 130,000 from the United Kingdom alone.[11] (See table 4.1.)

The economic effects of migration on a receiving country are complex and depend largely on the capital endowments that the migrants bring with them. If the immigrants are unskilled workers without capital, they will likely place downward pressure on the wages and, in some cases, the job prospects of native unskilled workers. That development, in turn, could undermine the domestic social compact. From the perspective of national welfare, then, growing inequality that can be attributed to migration may, as in the case of trade, have to be addressed by compensatory policies.

On the other hand, if the migrants are skilled and well endowed in capital, they may lower the returns to highly skilled workers and thereby contribute to a decrease in inequality; again, whether that is acceptable will depend on the nature of the domestic social compact. At the same time, the addition of these highly skilled migrant workers to the labor pool will increase the nation's capital stock and, as a consequence, its growth rate as well.

This does not mean that low-skilled workers would necessarily be rejected by capital-intensive economies on welfare grounds. As the World Bank economist Andrés Solimano suggests, "another channel through which migration can increase growth in the host country is by moderating the growth of wages . . . therefore contributing to keeping profits high, raising the profitability of *investment*, and accelerating growth. This is an *investment-led* growth mechanism. Another mechanism from migration to growth may operate through *savings*. As international migration tends to raise profits in receiving countries and profit-earners have a larger propensity to save than wage earners; the net result is an increase in overall national savings and an increase in growth."[12]

What are the economic effects on a developing country that loses workers through outward migration? Traditionally, scholars and policy makers have focused on the negative consequences of this flow, particularly because of the "brain drain." But the consequences are more nuanced then that phrase suggests, and can also cut in several different directions.

First, *by reducing the stock of high-skilled workers*, migration may actually contribute to narrowing inequality within poor countries. In this context, it is interesting to note that the reduction of income inequality is often held to be a worthwhile normative objective. But here is a case where the reduction may not serve the interests of lower-income groups. If high-skilled workers leave the country, for example, it may become less of a magnet for foreign direct investment, with the employment and technology such investment brings.[13] Further, by taking knowledge and capital away with them, migration of skilled labor may lower national growth rates by reducing the country's capital stock. And of greatest immediate importance to the poor, the reduction of high-skilled workers likely means fewer doctors, nurses, and teachers, ultimately restricting the opportunities to escape poverty and enjoy a better quality of life.

Second, in a more positive vein, *by sending part of their income back home* to their families, remittances can play a crucial role in supplementing the national savings rate. Indeed, remittances have become more important than foreign aid or direct investment as a source of external finance for many developing countries. As I will discuss in greater detail later, making these remittances work more effectively for development has become of increasing concern to the international community.

Third, outward migration of skilled workers may ultimately help the national economy, as these workers learn *new technologies and managerial techniques* that they can transfer back to their homelands. This phenomenon, for example, has had a positive impact on India's high-technology industries. Indeed, this is one of the reasons why "temporary work visas" in industrial countries are increasingly viewed as a "win-win" proposition, in that migrants learn new skills that they ultimately bring home with them.[14]

Finally, migration *may help to relieve population and unemployment pressures*. How all these various factors actually work out in terms of economic performance will depend on many country-specific variables.

Thinking about migration flows in terms of economic welfare as opposed to rights brings with it certain analytical advantages. First, it allows for easier comparisons between welfare in *both* sending and receiving countries. After all, it is not always straightforward to compare the domestic social compacts of two nations in ways that can be conveniently measured. Do British citizens migrate to the United States, for example, because they have fewer rights at home, or because their economic opportunities are greater in America? If the former is the case, how do we compare rights in Britain and America? If immigrants are primarily motivated by economic considerations, however, then income differences provide a useful proxy.

Second, the welfare perspective forces us to think more precisely about policy optimization at both the domestic and international levels. What are the economic effects of migration on sending and receiving countries? What changes in migration policy could make these flows a "win-win" proposition for all concerned? The answers to analytical questions of this type could be helpful to cosmopolitan, communitarian, and liberal internationalist theorists of international economic justice.

We should also note the several disadvantages of an economics-oriented approach to migration flows and policies. First, broad migration patterns obviously are not driven by economic factors alone. In the world of international politics, national security considerations, for instance, loom large. On a purely economic basis, for example, we would expect migration of unskilled labor from poor Arab states to Israel, and perhaps a flow of skilled labor in the opposite direction; that does not occur, of course, largely because of the military conflict in the region, and the public attitudes and government policies which that conflict creates.

Second, national immigration policies are often shaped by noneconomic factors. In the United States, for example, immigration policy is largely driven by family reunification, while in certain European countries the citizens of former colonies continue to have privileged access to the metropole. Economic criteria alone do not determine the immigration policies of many countries.

Third, rights matter. A fundamental difference between trade flows and migration is that people are endowed with rights. Indeed, it is impossible to have a meaningful debate over migration policy without recognizing the rights of all those involved. In the following sections, we will see how the rights and economic consequences associated with migration are assessed and balanced out by the communitarian, cosmopolitan, and liberal internationalist conceptions of justice.

National Welfare and Migration

The communitarian perspective on migration was pointedly summarized by the London *Economist* when it editorialized in 2002: "The first essential is to accept that the voters' right to a say about who and how many can enter *must take precedence* over the rights of those unlucky enough to be born in poorer parts of the world" (italics added).[15] No hint of prioritarian thought here! For the communitarian theorist, societies enter the global economy only to enhance their own well-being. Societies are therefore entitled to exclude those who might seek to enter the nation as migrants, or, more precisely, to allow entry only to those who are deemed to be positive contributors, say in economic terms, to the existing social compact.

But does this national welfare view necessarily point toward extreme limits on migration in the interest of preserving national identity? Not necessarily. Let us examine another, earlier editorial from the *Economist* on this same topic: "The absorptive capacity of Western European countries, though not as great as that of America or Australia, is still bigger than timid people think. European politicians who run scared of racist or anti-immigrant feeling will be doing their countries no favors. The guiding principle as they study Europe's immigration plans should not be 'How few can we get away with letting in?', but rather, 'How many can we possibly take without creating unbearable social strain?' "[16]

The reason for this position is not based on the rights of migrants, but rather on the economic needs of European countries that are faced with rapidly aging populations. This means that the dependency ratio (the ratio of retirees to workers) is rising, with fewer workers supporting more retirees, and that the natural birthrate is insufficient to change that outcome. Thus, migration is increasingly being looked to for its potential in addressing that problem. This reminds us again that economic pressures cannot be overlooked as we discuss migration policy.

Naturally, the national welfare theorist rejects any cosmopolitan vision of the "rights" of migrant persons to settle wherever they would like. For the communitarian, the existing social compact, grounded in a shared national identity, is a fragile one that migration could possibly disrupt. Myron Weiner defended the national welfare perspective in these terms:

> Any country, rich or poor, that opened its borders might soon find other states taking advantage of its beneficent policy. A neighboring country whose elite wanted a more homogeneous society could now readily expel its minori-

ties. A government that wanted a more egalitarian society could dump its unemployed and its poor. An authoritarian regime could rid itself of its opponents; a country could empty its jails, mental institutions, and homes for the aged. In an extreme case, an overcrowded populous country could take over a hypothetically generous country simply by "transferring" a large part of its population.[17]

Even if all migrants were highly desirable (say, because they were skilled), there might be legitimate reasons why societies would want to limit their entry. Michael Walzer notably argues that societies form closed political communities that can and should distinguish between "members" and "strangers." Walzer accepts the territorial state as a given in world politics, and suggests that the bond between a government and its people, the social compact, permits the state to regulate the flow of persons who define that political community. Distinctive political cultures *have* moral value for Walzer; they provide persons with codes of conduct and of behavior. We disrupt these distinctive cultures and political structures at our peril. To be sure, a given culture may choose more or less migration, and may define itself in more or less ethnically or religiously homogenous terms, but this should not influence our view of the justice of that particular social arrangement.[18]

In conclusion, then, a national welfare or communitarian theorist would judge the costs and benefits of migration in terms of migration's contribution to the maintenance of the domestic social compact. Some societies may look at this more or less in economic terms (e.g., Canada, which encourages immigration of those with high levels of wealth), while others will have strong ethnic or religious biases (e.g., Israel). So long as the "self-sufficient" political community is seen as the primary site of distributive justice, it is national migration policies that will determine the appropriate level of rights that outsiders should receive, and it will prove difficult for the international community to articulate a global migration policy.

Still, even in this case, the international community might wish to speak to the question of how migrants ought to be treated once they are admitted into a country. Just as corporations, for example, seek "national treatment" when they enter new markets, migrants—although not necessarily demanding citizen rights—will want to be assured equal treatment under the law and access to basic goods and services (e.g., education and health care).[19] And this claim on behalf of some set of minimal migrant rights naturally points us toward the cosmopolitan and liberal internationalist approaches to migration that we consider in the following sections.

Cosmopolitan Thought and Migration

For the cosmopolitan theorist, support for free international migration follows naturally from the position that only the individual has moral worth. Since the place of one's birth is morally arbitrary, and since place may exert a determinative role in one's life chances, free movement is a moral imperative. Further, from the perspective of a theory of personal freedom or universal human rights, free movement is consistent with the right of an individual to live and work wherever he or she pleases. Finally, from the cosmopolitan perspective of a truly borderless global economy, free migration is likely to reduce inequalities between peoples, to the extent that it reduces wage gaps between persons in sending and receiving nations. When people in low-wage countries migrate to high-wage economies, wages in the low-wage countries must rise and wages in the high-wage countries must fall.[20] As the economic historians Kevin O'Rourke and Jeffrey Williamson have written, "The convergence power of free migration, when it is tolerated, can be substantial."[21] Migration can therefore play a key role in promoting the cause of a more equitable global society.

In a 2002 essay, Rodrik provides a strong cosmopolitan case for free migration policy. He asks us to consider "the following thought experiment. Imagine that the negotiators who met recently in Doha to hammer out an agenda for world trade talks were really interested in boosting incomes around the world. . . . [T]he biggest bang by far lies in . . . relaxing restrictions on the international movement of workers."[22] Note that Rodrik's concern here is with boosting not the *national* incomes of developing countries but rather the incomes of *individuals*. Indeed, he emphasizes that "the economic benefits [of his policy proposal] would accrue directly to *workers* from developing nations rather than to their governments" (emphasis added).[23]

For cosmopolitans, international economic justice is found in treating each person as the member of a global polity to which they have equal rights. Under this view, it is very difficult to justify the exclusionary principle of migration that a communitarian theorist would adopt.[24] Since each and every person should have an equal right to the good life, and if that good life can only be found through migration, then such migration must be allowed in justice.

Yet economic analysis reveals some weaknesses with at least prioritarian versions of the theory of free migration. First, if the ultimate objective is to raise the incomes of those who are least advantaged, it is not obvious that a borderless world is necessarily the right solution. Roemer, for example, argues that, at some point, the open borders solution would be such as to reduce incomes for the least advantaged rather than to equalize them. He argues that welfare-oriented (as opposed to rights-based) cosmopolitans would actually want something less than open borders.[25]

Second, it is by no means clear that open borders would promote the life chances of the "least advantaged" or the poor who are currently living in poor countries. To begin with, it is generally not the poor who migrate; migration from developing countries actually rises with income levels, so that an African doctor is more likely to leave for Britain than an African farmer. Those who migrate from poor country S to rich country N are often the relatively wealthy or skilled in S, and the effects of this "brain drain" may be only a worsening of economic circumstances for the poor in S. This leads us to ask whether the ultimate value for cosmopolitans is promoting individual human rights or the welfare of the least advantaged.

As we have already seen in previous chapters, the cosmopolitan position and its prioritarian variant is very difficult to translate into policy practice. The process of identifying those who are least advantaged and encouraging their migration to wealthier states is by no means obvious, even if this policy were deemed desirable. But even the desirability of greater migration of poor persons to rich countries is debatable from at least a welfare perspective.

Still, the moral resonance of this position remains compelling, given the overwhelming influence of the place of one's birth on subsequent opportunities.

Liberal Internationalism and Migration

So what we have at this point are two normative frameworks that are not entirely satisfactory for dealing with the vexing problem of justice in migration. The communitarian theorist, concerned solely with his or her polity, fails to appreciate that the international community might take an interest in a host of migration-related problems. The cosmopolitan theorist, in contrast, questions the morality of associative relationships qua political communities, and therefore calls for migration policies that few societies are likely to contemplate. Further, it is not clear even from a prioritarian standpoint that free migration is the best solution if the objective is to improve the life chances of those who are least advantaged. This gridlock raises the question of whether a liberal internationalist, concerned with the interaction between the domestic and international social compacts, can make a useful contribution to the migration debate.

Once again, we begin to think about this issue by considering potential arrangements for building a fairer international migration regime, one that would be inclusive, participatory, and welfare-enhancing. From this perspective, there would seem to be some modest but nonetheless important cooperative steps that the international community could usefully and feasibly take. One of the major economic benefits of migration to developing countries, for example, is through flows of remittances. According to the International Organization for Migration (IOM), these remittances totaled more than seventy-two billion dollars in 2001, an amount that is larger than all the official development assistance flowing to the world's poorest nations. The IOM points out that these "remittances assist short-term poverty reduction. The majority of remittances are sent back to support family members and relatives, sometimes accounting for over 50% of the total household income."[26]

Unfortunately, these remittances are often costly to both migrants and their families. The banking system and other foreign exchange mechanisms take high fees for sending funds across borders and changing them into local currency. The IOM has proposed working with the international banking community to lower these fees, in an effort to ensure that the largest amount possible is remitted to the developing country.

In a similar vein, industrial and developing countries have disagreements over how worker remittances should be taxed across borders, that is, over the appropriate distribution of tax revenues. International tax treaties need to be forged that work for all countries concerned, and a trio of authors has argued that "such a regime has the potential for large and immediate revenue consequences for developing countries."[27] At present, there is little cooperation of this type. The international community can help make migration a system of mutual advantage by ensuring that higher remittance and tax flows reach families and source countries.

At some point, as previously noted, the international community might also wish to contemplate some minimal standards of migrant rights. Although countries will undoubtedly retain their own unique policies with respect to migrants and citizenship rights, these differences among states could generate flows of persons across borders, particularly in regions where cross-border transfers of persons are relatively easy, as in Western Europe or between Mexico and the United States. If one European state, for example, gives migrants relatively easy access to free education, health care, and welfare state insurance while another does not, it could induce migrants to move to the former. That sort of movement could become a source of tension between countries, and the international community might wish to avert such tensions by seeking a set of standards that all countries could agree on. Indeed, the ongoing debate over the European Constitution has involved, among many other issues, precisely these sorts of questions, and ultimately a minimal set of standards has been agreed on that may now be taken up in a new European Treaty should the Constitution be abandoned. If this concept of minimal migrant standards spreads internationally, they would likely have both "positive" and "negative" dimensions: positive obligations that states would assume toward migrant populations, such as access to health care, and negative constraints on state behavior and on that of other societal actors, so that the vulnerabilities of migrants—their relative lack of social and civil protections as compared to citizens—does not encourage economic agents to exploit them. Health and safety standards in the workplace, for example, should not differentiate between migrant and nonmigrant groups.

To conclude, justice in migration presents the society of states with one of its most difficult normative challenges. Differing conceptions of national identity and the domestic social compact make it difficult to imagine a global migration regime based on the principle of free migration of persons. At the same time, there is much the international system can usefully do to make migration a "win-win" proposition for all concerned. By promoting a minimal set of migrant rights and by facilitating remittance flows and achieving an equitable sharing of taxes, the society of states can act in positive ways to promote an international migration architecture that is of mutual advantage.

But migration hardly exhausts the issue of justice in labor. If states are unwilling to accept a completely free flow of migrants for fear of upsetting their domestic social compacts, the question arises of whether they are willing to do anything else to promote the living and working conditions of those in distant lands, especially people in developing countries. We turn to this question in the next section, where I discuss international labor standards.

Labor Standards and the Just Economy

The wealth of a nation is ultimately found in the productivity of its workers. Since work must be at the core of any public strategy to ensure economic justice, the fundamental labor policy of a fair society would be full employment.[28] Following Rawls, we can submit that just societies will do whatever is in their reasonable power to ensure that each and every individual has the opportunity to realize his or her talents within the labor market context. This has important domestic economic policy consequences; for John Maynard Keynes, it meant that "the State will have to exercise a guiding influence on the propensity to consume partly through its scheme of taxation, partly by fixing the rate of interest, and partly, perhaps, in other ways."[29]

But it is crucial to emphasize, as Keynes so powerfully reminded us during the 1930s, that full employment policies contribute to more than just the realization and maintenance of the *domestic* social compact. Full employment has significant *international* implications for prosperity as well. As Keynes wrote:

> if nations can learn to provide themselves with full employment by their domestic policy . . . there need be no important economic forces calculated to set the interest of one country against that of its neighbors. . . . There would still be room for the international division of labor. . . . But there would no longer be a pressing motive why one country need force its wares on another or repulse the offering of its neighbor. . . . International trade would not be what it is, namely, a desperate expedient to maintain employment at home by forcing sales on foreign markets and restricting purchases . . . *but a willing and unimpeded exchange of goods and services in conditions of mutual advantage.* [italics added][30]

How should full employment be defined and achieved? After all, people could simply be "put to work" by the state in a coercive fashion—as occurred in the former Communist societies—but in jobs that have little or nothing to do with their talents. In order to maximize efficiency while preserving individual freedom, labor policies would be designed to encourage the proper "match" between workers on the one hand and employers on the other, and this could require a host of supporting active labor market measures, including training and job placement services.

Clearly, different societies will have different approaches to achieving and even defining full employment.

Some will seek to achieve it through the market by urging that workers accept wage flexibility, while others will build a larger role for the state. Again, the international system will be host to a diversity of social compacts, and states will learn from one another's labor market experiments as they create full employment policies at home.

To be sure, the objective of full employment must be placed against other societal demands, such as the demand for "fair" wages or safe working conditions. Workers who seek a minimum wage, the right of association through unions or work councils, or better health and safety standards, could undermine a society's full employment goal by raising the price of labor. In other words, a society's precise definition of "full employment" will be contingent on these other values and variables as well.

Further, there is the important question of who should participate in the labor market. In many societies, for example, children are denied access to the labor market until they reach school-leaving age, and women are kept from performing certain kinds of jobs, for example in mines, military combat units, or other dangerous occupations. As Rodrik has written, "Nations do have collective preferences over what kinds of production technologies are admissible ("fair" or "legitimate"), and governments have always had restrictions on technologies that violate these boundaries, even on those that promise a large increase in a nation's productive potential. The ban on slave labor is, of course, the example that comes immediately to mind."[31]

When we speak of the broad set of policies that are meant to "decommodify" labor or remove it from market dictates, we often refer to "labor standards." But let us be clear what is meant by labor standards. In fact, the concept incorporates two distinct notions, one largely procedural, the other consequentialist. Under the procedural view, labor standards consist mainly of rules and regulations that provide labor with a "level playing field" in its negotiations with capital. Given a competitive market economy at full employment, for example, employers offer jobs at certain wages, and workers responding by taking up or refusing those positions. So long as neither agent has monopoly power over the other, the negotiation must be deemed fair by both sides.

In situations where full employment does not obtain, however, or where the capital-labor balance is somehow tilted against one or the other party, institutions may be required to facilitate agreements that are deemed to be of mutual advantage. In the absence of such mediating institutions, the domestic social compact could be undermined as raw monopoly power is exploited in order to extract rents from those who are most vulnerable.

Consequentialists, in contrast, would conceptualize labor standards in terms of some specific set of outcomes or patterns that society deems to be minimally acceptable. These could include minimum wages, health and safety standards, hours of work, and the like. The consequentialist's main concern is therefore with developing and articulating the outcomes that the members of a just society would generally deem to be acceptable, in labor among other issues.

For a liberal such as Rawls, the task of drawing up a set of fair or just labor standards would be complicated by his two broad principles of justice that well-ordered societies must meet. The first principle of justice requires a system of equal liberties for all, while the second demands a difference principle that seeks to maximize opportunities for

TABLE 4.2
Types of Labor Standards

Type	Examples
1. Human rights	Prohibitions on slave labor
2. Civic rights	Rights to free association
3. Survival rights	Rights to a "living wage"
4. Security rights	Rights to worker's compensation

Source: Adapted from Keith Maskus, "Should Core Labor Standards Be Imposed through International Trade Policy?" (manuscript, prepared for the World Bank, International Trade Division, August 1997), p. 8.

those who are least advantaged. In the first case, labor standards, if they were deemed necessary by society, would have to be universal, such that no "privileged" or "aristocratic" group of workers, no closed union shops, could emerge, unless it was argued that such a labor market structure was to *everyone's* advantage. And the difference principle suggests that any labor standards that were adopted would have to be designed in such as way as to promote the life chances of, say, the poor, the handicapped, or those who are least-advantaged. A minimum wage that effectively closes the job market to unskilled workers by reducing demand for their services would not necessarily be consistent with Rawlsian justice.

In practice, the phrase *core labor standards* (CLS) as commonly used refers to a mix of processes and outcomes. Thus, the economist Keith Maskus has conceptualized labor standards as set out in table 4.2. As we can see, the divisions among CLS are not necessarily clear-cut. Security rights and survival rights may be confused, and some would claim that certain civic rights are basic human rights. Further, some of the CLS, such as survival rights, are mainly concerned with outcomes, whereas civic rights are more focused on processes. Keeping in mind this distinction between procedures and outcomes is useful in contemplating the nature of fair labor standards.

Justice in International Labor Standards

It is one thing to impose labor standards at home, consistent with the domestic social compact. But what if society N finds the "low" labor standards in society S contrary to its values? Or, to put this in economic terms, what if the labor standards in S create a "negative externality" for N?

This externality could take several forms. First, N might find the "slave" wages, long working hours, or unsafe working conditions in S morally disturbing. Second, N might believe that the low labor standards in S were making it difficult, given international competition, to maintain its own set of high labor standards. Third, N might believe that S's low labor standards were preventing the implementation of higher standards in countries X, Y, and Z, or even promoting a "race to the bottom" among them. For any of these reasons, the domestic social compacts in N and S could come into conflict, leading to the question of how the international community should respond.

It has long been argued that this sort of dynamic, also known as "social dumping," is an unfortunate feature of the global economy, requiring international cooperative action in response. As Herbert Feis wrote during the 1930s, "Those interested in the improvement of industrial conditions in various countries had more than once found that a desired change in labor conditions was hindered by the possibility that the same industry in some other country might secure a competitive advantage as a result. . . . The idea of resorting to joint international action is, therefore, natural in such contingencies."[32]

There are several ways in which N could respond to S's low standards. First, it could unilaterally impose trade sanctions on S's exports. Second, it could ask the international community to create some multilateral set of core labor standards that would be enforced collectively through trade or other sanctions. The international community's response to South African apartheid comes to mind as a prominent example of collective action in the face of a globally perceived injustice. Finally, N could offer to pay for higher standards in S through the provision of foreign aid, or by providing open markets for its goods; these policies rely on "carrots" rather than "sticks." Let us explore each of these policies in turn.

There is now a voluminous economics literature on the relationship between so-called core labor standards and the international trade regime. This is because most of the policy (and activist) focus in this debate has emphasized the possibility of linking the demand for higher labor standards with the threat of trade sanctions.[33] Most economists have argued that this approach should be avoided.[34] They do not believe that trade should be made hostage to higher labor (or environmental) standards, and that these issues should be "delinked" in international negotiations.[35]

Economists come to this view for several reasons. First, they doubt whether low labor standards in relatively unproductive developing countries do in fact undermine high standards in technologically advanced industrial countries. There is simply no evidence, for example, that multinational enterprises locate their operations in particular countries *because* of low labor standards. To the contrary, foreign direct investment gravitates mainly toward wealthy markets and their highly skilled workers. The main developing country recipients of foreign direct investment, such as China and Brazil, have large internal markets that make operations there attractive; again, low labor standards do not provide a source of competitive advantage.

Second, economists fear that linking trade policy and labor standards represents the proverbial wolf in sheep's clothing, in that protectionist interests would use the labor standards debate simply as a way of keeping imports out of a high-standard country. To the extent that labor standards reflect a nation's level of overall wealth, most economists would argue that it is better for a state to trade and become wealthier, and in that way induce higher standards, rather than sanction and keep the targeted nation in poverty.

Finally, economists would argue that the choice of labor standards is for a particular society to decide, given its level of economic development and the nature of its social compact. For all these reasons, the idea of coercing higher labor standards through trade sanctions and the denial of market access has not won widespread academic support.

But these economic arguments are not our primary concern. Instead, the issue we must confront is whether or not some core set of international labor standards—like the core standards of the International Labor Organization, which, among other things, forbid child labor and accept the right to organize and to bargain collectively—would be agreed on *and enforced* by the society of states in the name of building a fairer global economy. Conversely, we need to ask whether the individual members of the society of states, who have developed a given set of standards for their own domestic purposes, could in justice coerce other nations into adopting some allegedly "cosmopolitan" or "universal" set of standards. I will argue that the society of states would likely avoid coercive solutions to the labor standards issue in most cases. In making this argument, we must recall that international economic justice is found in an arrangement that is participatory, inclusive, and, welfare-enhancing, with special consideration for poor or developing countries.

Because it is such an emotionally charged issue, it is worth exploring the problem of child labor as a case study of international labor standards. After all, few readers of this book would wish to have their children working long hours in factories or shops, and, as already mentioned, an international prohibition on child labor already exists. The best thing for children, of course, is to stay in school, acquiring the skills that are needed to increase their future opportunity set and earnings capacity.

But in many countries, poor kids do not stay in school, and for them employment may be better than the next best alternative, including street crime and prostitution. Yet this has not stopped some activists from seeking to enforce a ban on child labor. During the 1990s, for example, what might be called an "ethics crusade" was launched against the major manufacturers of soccer balls, including Reebok and Nike, because their suppliers used child labor in home manufacturing in Pakistani villages. The outcome of this public industrial-world outcry was the decision to eliminate these suppliers and to build instead a brand-new manufacturing facility.

Unfortunately, the community that once made the soccer balls suffered when the suppliers left town, and today it is left without its manufacturing and economic base, and there are no greater educational opportunities for the local workers, including children.[36] The international community expressed its outrage about child labor but did not accept the responsibility that followed from that expression by caring for the children who had been displaced as a result. In a nontrivial sense, the outcry represented "cheap talk," because nobody was prepared to help finance the education or other alternatives for those who had been displaced once the soccer ball manufacturing ceased.

In the absence of external assistance, countries may have to "grow" their way out of child labor; the fact is that as countries move out of poverty, child labor tends to decrease. And the best way out of poverty for most countries is through trade. Sanctioning a poor country, without providing any carrots, could well prove counterproductive.[37]

Does this mean that no ethical case can be made for international labor standards? Hardly, but such standards are most useful when they are part of a broader international development *strategy*, that is, an integrated approach to growth-enhancing policies that incorporates trade, aid, and other programs. Labor standards, for example, have been used by the United States and the European Union as a carrot, in which countries—say, Cambodia, to cite a specific example—that adopt higher standards receive greater market access for exports such as textiles in return.[38]

I am, in contrast, skeptical—as I believe many governments of developing countries are—of labor standards that serve as a sort of normative, stand-alone "checklist" by which we judge and even sanction a country's social compact, allowing for exceptions such as prohibitions against slave labor, which is now universally condemned (and even in this case we must recognize that slavery remains a scourge—think of sex trafficking—with few sanctions imposed on countries that allow it to continue). On such a stand-alone basis, most international labor standards would be difficult to enforce in a world of diverse societies whose policies reflect differing social compacts and levels of political and economic development. Further, labor standards, even if they were to be imposed from the outside, may not benefit those who are least advantaged, that is, the very persons who are the object of much of the normative attention. To the contrary, to the extent that higher standards lead to job displacement from the formal to the informal sectors, they could make the plight of the poor even worse. As a consequence, an "economic dualism" arises in the labor market, segmenting privileged and informal-sector workers.[39]

In contrast, labor standards can play a useful role when they are part of a broader policy commitment to the growth of developing countries, and more research is needed to consider what an "optimal" package of standards and other growth-inducing policies would look like.[40] Generally, these standards can help move countries and firms toward higher-productivity undertakings and away from the rut of low-wage, low-productivity manufacturing. In that sense, standards that protect, say, the health and safety of workers, can be usefully conceptualized as a "public good," in that they have economywide benefits. To the extent the international community seeks the development of its poorest and least-advantaged member states, it should stand willing to work with them in articulating and helping to finance the sorts of standards that can be shown to bring such positive social gains. In this context, it is of interest to note that the very earliest international labor standards, written at the end of the nineteenth century, were concerned with the health and safety of labor.

In conclusion, labor standards generally arise out of the domestic social compact rather than from some universal or shared conception of what constitutes the good life, and reflect the preferences and trade-offs of national societies concerning employment, economic development, and other variables. Certainly, shared normative ideas do arise and spread over time as states learn from one another about what labor-market institutions and regulations are best suited to advancing the social compact that they wish to perfect. Still, it must be recognized that even among the advanced industrial countries, very different policy approaches to labor markets have been adopted. The Europeans, for example, seem to have a greater tolerance for unemployment than do Americans, who accept a greater degree of job and wage flexibility. Perhaps these labor market institutions will converge over time, but significant national differences will likely remain. Attempts to impose or coerce global labor standards, therefore, will rarely find a place in a just international system; in contrast, efforts to improve working conditions through the "carrots" of aid and trade and the exchange of "best practices" should be welcomed.

Conclusions

Labor markets form a crucial link between the international and domestic social compacts. As we have seen in this chapter, however, the establishment of justice in labor at the domestic and international levels poses analytical challenges of the highest magnitude. Domestically, labor markets that, say, ensure high wages to union members may also produce low wages or high unemployment among "outsiders." Internationally, efforts to globalize labor standards through coercion could end up hurting those who are least advantaged, such as the poor in developing countries.

I have argued that each national polity must take primary responsibility for its labor markets, including its policies on migration and labor standards. That does not mean, however, that the international community will have no role to play in these debates. To the extent that the members of the society of states seek agreements on labor and migration that are inclusive, participatory, and welfare-enhancing, they will find that a politically feasible set of such policies in these areas can be generated. Such policies would facilitate worker remittances and a fair division of tax revenues.

Going further, fruitful international discussions could revolve around the relationship between labor standards and development. To put this more sharply, countries that care about higher labor standards should embed them in development strategy, and not simply impose them in "checklist" fashion. To be sure, these are modest contributions to a complex and emotional set of issues, but they suggest that the international system need not produce an economic "race to the bottom" that inevitably harms the poorest countries and those workers who are least advantaged within them. Given the gravity of these issues, we should seize the opportunities to move forward in justice wherever we find them.

5

HARNESSING INVESTMENT

Drawing a connection between multinational enterprises and international justice
is no easy task.
—Debora Spar and David Yoffie

For better or worse, governments provide the global economy with its authoritative normative structure and operating principles. But the sources of those norms are diverse, and the norms themselves are often contested. Human rights, for example, now occupy a central place on the international agenda, thanks to the work of nongovernmental organizations (NGOs) such as Amnesty International and Human Rights Watch, and environmental groups have played a key role in raising public consciousness about issues such as climate change and biodiversity. These examples suggest that norms are fluid and amenable to change.

Among the NGOs that shape global economic norms, none are as significant as the multinational enterprise (MNE). It is MNEs that generate the vast majority of the world's trade and investment flows, and that dominate global production and distribution networks. Harnessing the multinational in the interests of developing countries has therefore been a long-standing concern of both students and practitioners of globalization. As Thomas Franck has written, "the gap between developed and developing countries is so central an element of the fairness problematic that it must be addressed not only in terms of state-to-state action but also in terms of the interaction between private investors in developed economies and the governments of states which receive overseas investment."[1]

Whether the MNE contributes to or detracts from the realization of a level playing field for global economic transactions has been a major topic of debate among academics, policy makers, and activists for many decades.[2] Indeed, because of their alleged power, MNEs were constantly exposed to the threat or reality of nationalization and expropriation for much of the postwar era.[3] Today, in contrast, states are scrambling to attract foreign direct investment (FDI). That is not altogether surprising, in that "the most important source of development capital for poor countries is the private sector of rich ones."[4]

In thinking about the relationship between states and MNEs, one critical difference between these actors must be highlighted at the outset: the authority of governments is defined by territorial frontiers, whereas that of multinational enterprises is not. According to some observers, this structural difference gives the firms an "unfair" advantage over governments in the bargaining process over market access.[5] Just as mobile capital is able to "exploit" an immobile workforce in wage negotiations, so too the MNE can allegedly extract concessions from developing-world governments in the form of weak labor and environmental regulations, low taxes, and other subsidies. As governments are pitted against one another by firms in an effort to attract and keep FDI, a "race to the bottom" ensues in which the costs associated with subsidizing the MNE's activities outweigh the economic benefits that the country receives in terms of job creation, export earnings, tax revenues, and technology transfer.

But the flip side of this perspective emphasizes the power of governments to establish or to change the terms of an investment once it has been made. Governments may renege on agreements they have reached, changing the tax treatment that firms receive or even threatening to expropriate or nationalize their investments. Thus, governments may act in ways that we could judge to be unfair as well. Again to cite Franck, "an investor should feel confident of being at an equilibrium with the contracting government rather than at its mercy. This seems the essence of *law as fairness*" (italics added).[6]

This chapter considers relations between multinational firms and developing-world governments, and what might constitute a level playing field between them. I do not address the panoply of "moral" or "ethical" issues that individual multinational managers may face in particular countries, such as corruption, which have received substantial treatment elsewhere.[7] Nor do I discuss what a fair allocation of FDI *among* countries would look like, although I do take up the ongoing problem of investment subsidies. Although it is undoubtedly the case that very little FDI enters the developing world beyond Brazil, China, and a handful of other countries, I cannot conceive of any centrally directed, global allocation of foreign investment or of subsidies that would do much to promote the cause of a more just global economy.

A useful role for the international community, in contrast, is to provide technical assistance to help *all* governments establish the appropriate policy frameworks in order to attract FDI, assuming that they wish to receive it; indeed, this was one of the initial purposes of the

World Bank. Furthermore, trade policies in industrial countries should be designed to encourage foreign investment in developing ones. As I have already pointed out in earlier chapters, tariff escalation by the United States and the European Union—or raising tariff levels as commodities become processed (e.g., from coffee beans to instant coffee)—discourages value-added investment in many regions and as a consequence reduces their chances for growth.

In this chapter I advance the argument that negotiations between multinational firms and host countries are usefully conceptualized as a search for a level playing field. However, that search presents serious challenges to both parties, since each side necessarily wants to maximize the benefits and minimize the costs associated with FDI. Because FDI is "lumpy," the parties will tend to discount the value of future agreements and will try to get the most advantage they can out of each specific deal. Further, they will be tempted to change the terms of the bargains they have already reached when the moment is ripe to do so. Unlike trade negotiations among states, which may assume a more or less infinite time horizon, and which therefore are more likely to induce cooperative outcomes, it will be difficult to define bargains between firms and governments that each side views as being fair. From a game-theoretic perspective, the shadow of the future is longer in trade than in FDI, making tit-for-tat cooperation among trading partners easier to realize than it is among investors and recipients.

Owing to the special difficulties involved in reaching fair bargains in FDI, recent years have seen both governments and firms alike seek to elaborate codes of conduct and bilateral and multilateral investment treaties. My argument is that these codes and treaties represent an effort to nest specific investment decisions within a broader normative framework—one that is more participatory, inclusive, and welfare-enhancing. The purpose of this exercise is to lengthen the shadow of the future surrounding FDI, thereby creating a more cooperative environment in which bargaining can take place. Still, the international community has a very far distance to travel in that direction.

Bargaining between States and Firms: Beyond One-Shot Deals

The multinational is hardly a new actor on the global economic stage. Although we might debate whether its roots are found in the Dutch East Indies Company or the Standard Oil Trust, national firms with specific advantages have long sought to profit by investing overseas.[8] To be sure, the relationship between MNEs and developing countries has not been a naturally harmonious one. MNEs have allegedly bribed local governments for market access on a regular basis and, where acceptable arrangements could not be made or maintained, have sometimes sought support from the intelligence services and armed forces of their home governments. MNEs have tried to minimize or even evade taxes through the use of creative accounting techniques and transfer pricing mechanisms. They have also been accused of supporting authoritarian regimes over democratic ones, since the former have been less inclined to empower workers through unionization or collective bargaining.[9]

Conversely, MNEs have also confronted a variety of unsavory governments as they ventured overseas. The prevalence of corruption needs little emphasis, though perhaps we would do well to remember that "it takes two to tango," and until recently governments such as Germany's have allowed their corporations to deduct from federal taxes the direct payments made to local officials in order to provide market access. Rulers of many developing countries have also used the receipts from FDI as personal cash flow as opposed to financing for development, with the result that these funds have enjoyed a first-class trip to Switzerland rather than an extended stay in the host country.

Notwithstanding the checkered history of FDI, from a theoretical perspective at least it appears that transactions between investors and national governments could be readily conceptualized as relations of mutual advantage. Foreign investment brings with it critical assets in the form of financial, technological, and human resources, and income streams in the form of wages to workers, purchases from local suppliers, and tax payments to national and municipal governments. There are also significant externalities generated by multinational firms, often in the form of the technical training and know-how they provide to local workers. These externalities diffuse through the local economy, as the workers from MNE eventually leave for domestic firms with the knowledge they have gained (to the extent that such knowledge is not firm-specific), raising productivity levels. At the same time, MNEs will often invest in public goods, including roads, schools, and hospitals, if only because this provides the necessary infrastructure for their workforce and operations.

Despite all the benefits associated with FDI, relations between firms and governments have often been conflicted. Why is that the case? The late (and great) Charles

Kindleberger put his finger on the problem in a series of lectures he gave in 1968. The "antagonism between host country and investing company" is found simply in the fact that "their interests diverge."[10]

But how can interests diverge when the relations between states and firms are of mutual advantage? Again, to cite Kindleberger, the problem is that both parties "are interested in bigger pies, but for a pie of any given size, more for one means less for the other."[11] As we can see, the conflicts between these actors are primarily distributive in nature; fundamentally, they are about distributive justice.

The bargaining process between states and firms that determines relative shares of the pie might be tilted in one direction or another because of some decisive advantage that a party brings to the table. Host countries have the advantage of controlling the territory and the national markets that investors wish to access. But multinational firms may have specific knowledge with respect to the technologies that they will bring with them and the real costs of production, not to mention the bargaining power they possess that is associated with their ability to locate operations in one country or another. As the pie gets divided, the multinationals may use their specific knowledge of cost structures to engage in transfer pricing in such a way as to minimize profits, and thus tax payments to the host country. Each side—government and firm— will therefore bring to the bargaining table some a priori ideas concerning which side holds the strongest hand.[12]

It is precisely because the bargains between firms and governments involve questions of distributive justice that words such as *exploitation*, on the one hand, and *fairness*, on the other, come readily to the minds of scholars working in this field. Thus, in a famous article, Edith Penrose accused the then British-controlled Iraq Petroleum Company of "exploiting" the Iraqi government because it had received what appeared to her as highly favorable concession terms.[13] To her, a "fair" agreement would have been one that provided the company with the *minimum acceptable return* while still operating the oil concession.

Indeed, as Kindleberger points out, the oil industry offers an "instructive example" of fairness questions in investment. During the postwar years, as producing countries observed the high profits that the oil companies were making from their investments, governments sought time and again to renegotiate the terms of their profit-sharing arrangements. I cite Kindleberger at length, because the point he makes is so cogent to the argument of this chapter:

> In Venezuela, expanding production led to the adoption of the 50-50 agreement between companies and host governments, which was gradually extended to the Middle East. Under the formula, the sum of royalties and profits was divided 50-50 between company and host government. . . . *The 50-50 rule had a ring of fairness and equal sharing about it* [italics added]. In bargaining and non-zero-sum game theory, solutions come to rest on formulations that are widely familiar. . . . *The companies hoped that they could hold the line at 50-50 because of its self-evident fairness—though they conceded it has no validity as a market-clearing price* [italics added].[14]

Kindleberger provides other examples from the oil industry where the search for a fair deal has proved elusive. In constructing the Trans-Arabian Pipeline (TAPLINE) that ran from Saudi Arabia to Lebanon, for example, the governments concerned had to negotiate a tariff structure. As the outlet to the Mediterranean, Lebanon thought that it should be rewarded for its strategic location, but because the bulk of the pipeline ran through Saudi Arabia, Riyadh wanted payment on a per-mile basis. For their part, Iraq and Syria argued that the countries involved should share equally in the TAPLINE's profits. This sort of debate is about distributive or economic justice and "to the economist, the sad thing is that there is no basis . . . for saying that one view is more nearly right than another."[15]

This problem of what constitutes a fair division of rents usefully brings us back to game theory and a bargaining framework. As I discussed earlier in this book, cooperation becomes increasingly difficult to achieve as the "shadow of the future" shortens, that is, when an arrangement is viewed as a "one-shot deal" instead of an iterated sequence of bargains that stretch into the indefinite future. With respect to any particular investment decision, each side will seek to maximize its share of the profits. Kindleberger quite accurately asserted, "If countries and companies were to operate on long-run principles of cooperation and even-dealing, the outcome would be positive gains on both sides. But either company or host country may be greedy . . . and move to short-run maximization. . . . How does one make peace when the other wants war?"[16]

Further, host countries may be tempted to change the terms of any agreement once the FDI has been made; for this reason, Raymond Vernon famously called FDI an "obsolescing bargain."[17] As James Markusen has written, "Once the investment is made, the host country can renege on tax or other agreements, and directly or indirectly expropriate rents from the MNE."[18]

Game-theoretic models suggest that cooperation ob-
tains more easily when actors are playing an iterated as
opposed to a one-shot game.[19] In terms of foreign direct
investment, lengthening the shadow of the future is difficult, given the lumpy nature of investment decisions, and
can only be done by "nesting" specific investments within
a broader normative framework that governs relations between multinational firms and host countries, in other
words, by creating what might be called "institutions."[20]

By creating institutions (interpreted broadly to mean
formal or informal rules and standards, including legal
agreements, that agents adopt and that guide their behavior), any single investment may be transformed from a
one-off event into part of a future and indeterminate
stream of investment flows. The objective of each party
will then be to maximize the benefits associated with these
flows. Again to cite Kindleberger, "A way out of the dilemma posed by . . . tactical questions is often sought in
the adoption of rules," since rules help structure *future*
interactions.[21]

Given the strategic context between states and firms, it
becomes readily understandable why recent years have
seen a wide-ranging debate among national governments,
international organizations, and MNEs with respect to
the rules that are needed to govern FDI. Today, a dense
network of both formal rules and informal codes of conduct can be found that seek to shape the terms of FDI at
many different levels.

Thus, the United Nations' Global Compact asks multinational firms to adhere to the United Nations' core principles with respect to human rights, labor standards, and
environmental protection. From a more operational
standpoint, the Organization for Economic Cooperation

and Development (OECD) has a long-standing set of Guidelines for Multinational Enterprises that detail the appropriate expectations that governments may have of firms with respect to tax payments, technology transfer, and the like; and the OECD recently sought, unsuccessfully, to implement a new Multilateral Agreement on Investment (MAI). These initiatives are discussed in greater detail in the next sections. Governments have also implemented a variety of bilateral, regional, and multilateral investment treaties. Again, an objective of all these rules and codes is to nest specific investments within a broader normative framework, thereby lengthening the shadow of the future and making cooperation between states and firms more feasible.

Governing the Multinational Enterprise— and the State

If a one-shot investment game is to be transformed into long-term cooperative play, how is that best accomplished? Game theory suggests that the principle of reciprocity must play a key role. James Markusen has stated the case well. He argues that the move to create international codes and rules for investment has very little to do "with the economists' concept of welfare."[22] Whereas *unilateral* opening to FDI would likely be welfare-enhancing in most cases, reciprocity among states provides a better foundation for building a more robust and cooperative market access regime. Significantly for our purposes, Markusen asserts that "closely related" to this idea of reciprocity-based cooperation in investment "is the concept of 'fairness.' Rules are designed to promote . . . fairness in the international market place, which is often consistent with efficiency, though not necessarily so."[23]

What constitutes fairness in investment? A fundamental principle is "national treatment," the idea that a foreign firm should be treated exactly the same as a domestic one. To be sure, foreign firms may say they want national treatment but are then happy to profit from the special incentives offered to MNEs by governments in the form of tax holidays and other subsidies. Unfortunately, such schemes can tilt the playing field in favor of the MNE when compared to domestic firms, a situation that the latter will undoubtedly view as being unfair to them. By attracting foreign investment through subsidies that give multinational firms a competitive advantage over domestic ones, governments risk upsetting their country's domestic social compact, the basic agreement between state and society, and we can therefore understand why the issue of FDI is so fraught with controversy in many markets around the world.

In seeking to level the playing field between governments and firms as they negotiate market access agreements, codes of conduct have been part of the international landscape for at least the past thirty years. For much of this time, the source of unfairness was thought to be found in the firm's economic power and transnational character. During the 1970s and 1980s, for example, the United Nations and its Conference on Trade and Development (UNCTAD) made several ill-fated attempts at devising codes of conduct that would be binding on multinational firms. As Edward Graham has written, "The basic assumption behind all of these codes was that multinational firms were inherently likely to behave in a manner contrary to the interests of developing countries, and that the world needed enforceable rules to temper this behavior."[24]

Only more recently would it occur to governments that perhaps *they* also had to be subject to codes of conduct with respect to *their* behavior toward foreign investors—and indeed toward one another, as investment subsidies have provoked a race to the bottom among states (more on this later). And with FDI increasing in importance to developing countries, home and host governments have signed any number of bilateral investment treaties (BITs) aimed at providing some rules of the game for all parties.

But BITs have not solved the problem of investment competition *among* states. That would require a multilateral regulatory agreement. A review of the ill-fated Multilateral Agreement on Investment is suggestive of the problems associated with building a durable framework of that type in this issue area.

The MAI represented an attempt by the member governments of the OECD—in short, the advanced industrial countries—to draw up an accord among themselves that would govern FDI. Since developing countries do not belong to the OECD, they were not formally involved in the negotiation process, although some countries (e.g., Brazil) served as observers; the talks, therefore, were neither inclusive nor broadly participatory, at least from the standpoint of the *recipients* of FDI. Since most FDI is sourced out of OECD member states, the idea was to achieve a high standard that industrial-world governments might wish to adopt in regulating the behavior of their firms.[25] However, OECD members could not reach final agreement and the MAI died. Whether its demise was to the detriment of developing countries' interests, despite their lack of representation, remains a topic of debate.

The MAI included the following key provisions:

1. The "right of establishment" for foreign investors;

2. The principle of "most-favored nation" (MFN) treatment in investment, so that foreign companies, no matter their home country, have equal access to host country markets;

3. The principle of "national treatment," so that foreign companies are treated equally to domestic ones;

4. Investment protection against expropriation;

5. Abolition of specific performance requirements on MNEs, such as meeting export targets or technology transfer objectives; and

6. Rules and procedures for dispute settlement between MNEs and host governments.[26]

It is notable that the one item *not* taken up by the OECD members in their MAI talks was perhaps the most significant item when it came to enhancing their own welfare and that of developing-country recipients of FDI, and that was the treatment of investment subsidies. As Graham writes, "The omission of investment incentives from the MAI is arguably the agreement's most blatant deficiency in terms of its ability to alter the practices of governments that might have adverse effects on the outcome of investment decisions. It probably is the most intractable as well, given that the problem has the nature of a prisoner's dilemma."[27]

What Graham meant, of course, is that each state has an interest in limiting or eliminating the investment subsidies it provides to MNEs, but each state also wants to win more FDI. Since there is no external enforcement agency to limit competition among states, the players engage in a race to the bottom, providing more subsidies than they would like, to the benefit of foreign investors but to the detriment of the states themselves. Perhaps more powerfully than any other case in this book, investment subsidies demonstrate the continuing challenges of creating an international economy that is truly welfare enhancing, given the anarchic structure of world politics.

All things being equal, the subsidies game can only "benefit" the country with the deepest pockets (although this country suffers lost tax revenues as well), providing an important source of unfairness in the global economy. And it is notable in this context that even the "liberal" hegemonic power, the United States, which has stressed the importance of international economic rules for trade and finance and invested so much in building a multilateral system of governance in these areas, has done next to nothing to prevent this sort of race for investment dollars from occurring, even within its own borders. To the contrary, the various states engage in such heated competition for investment that the Federal Reserve Bank of Minneapolis has published a manifesto arguing that "Congress Should End the Economic War among the States."[28]

As the late Raymond Vernon wrote in his last book:

> The use of subsidies in the international competition for multinational enterprises continues to have a very strong potential for the generation of tensions. At least three obstacles will have to be overcome, however, in order to frame an effective agreement in this area. One is the resistance of the multinational enterprises themselves, which can only gain from the competitive offerings of different countries. Another obstacle is the resistance of the subnational units in many countries . . . whose internecine com-

petition accounts for a major part of the international flow of subsidies. And a final obstacle is the resistance that some countries will offer to the creation of any new international machinery required for effective enforcement of an agreement limiting the use of subsidies.[29]

Even taking the investment subsidies issue out of the MAI package, one might argue, as Graham has effectively done, that the agreement, however incomplete, would still have been in the interest of at least most of the developing countries that seek foreign investment, despite their lack of formal participation in the deliberations. It would have leveled important parts of the playing field and in so doing would have left the subsidies issue more exposed, to be dealt with at a later time, one would hope. That also holds true for another important topic left out of the MAI, transfer pricing, in which MNEs allocate costs among their subsidiaries in such a way as to minimize the corporate tax burden and maximize profits. These reservations aside, the MAI would have produced a more transparent regime for FDI, providing a basis upon which future intergovernmental negotiations could have been built, and, in turn, a sturdier normative framework for relations between host countries and MNEs.

In this context, it is ironic that many NGOs took up the cudgel against the MAI. Oxfam—always ready to speak on behalf of developing countries and the poor—was a leading opponent of the agreement. It argued against the national treatment provisions of the MAI and in favor of continued specific performance requirements—even in light of strong economic evidence that such requirements are "counterproductive." This is because multinational firms may be reluctant to invest anything at all in countries that impose strong performance requirements, many of which cannot be fulfilled in any event.[30] Achieving an export-performance target, for example, depends, among other things, on the state of the world economy. Oxfam further argued that any MAI must include international labor and environmental standards, even though, as I have argued in earlier chapters, developing countries themselves have balked at the imposition of such standards, seeing them as industrial-world protectionism in disguise, rather than any commitment to raising their productivity and economic growth.[31]

In sum, the failure of the MAI may be viewed as a setback for the establishment of an international regime governing FDI. That setback is not altogether surprising, given the difficulty of lengthening the shadow of the future when investment decisions are "lumpy" and time-limited. With overwhelming temptations by both states and firms to view each investment decision as a one-shot deal rather than as part of an iterated relationship, it becomes difficult to strike cooperative agreements that each side views as being fair. Unlike trade between states, which consists of an entire range of goods and services that are exchanged over long periods of time, investment negotiations focus on specific transactions. In this setting, it is difficult to lengthen the shadow of the future.

At the same time, a dense network of bilateral investment treaties now governs FDI, and these may provide the basis for future multilateral negotiations. But meaningful policy efforts will have to focus on unfair competition in subsidies and the transfer pricing that almost certainly limits tax payments to certain host countries, especially in the developing world.[32] As these points make clear, we still have a long way to go in bringing justice to investment at the international level.

Private Standards and Corporate Social Responsibility

Given the failure of governments to negotiate binding international codes on FDI, NGOs and other societal actors have stepped into the breach and turned their attention directly to the MNE. This is a logical evolution. If governments cannot reach international agreements, then the second best—and perhaps even first best—solution is to get the MNEs themselves, whose operations naturally span national borders, to implement corporatewide codes of conduct and standards of behavior. Thus, if the United States, France, and China cannot agree, for example, on international labor or environmental standards, it makes sense for nongovernmental actors to lobby the MNEs operating in these markets to adopt them instead—or to shame them into doing so, using the media as necessary to reveal "unethical" behavior on the part of these firms. In this way, corporate social responsibility may be seen as a euphemism for government regulatory failures. As John Gerard Ruggie has written, "as governments have been creating the space for trans-national corporations to operate globally, other social actors have sought to infuse that space with greater corporate social obligations."[33]

Today, firms are being called upon by these actors, in the name of corporate social responsibility, not only to set high labor and environmental standards, but to provide a wide variety of goods and services to the countries in which they invest, ranging from training programs for workers to infrastructure programs to the provision, in the case of pharmaceutical companies, of donated drugs.

Ironically, firm performance is being monitored on these broader, nonfinancial grounds not so much by host governments in developing countries, but by institutional investors, NGOs, and other "stakeholders" in the rich, industrial world. These stakeholders have proposed a nearly endless variety of corporate, sectoral, and broader business standards that firms are expected to meet if they wish to be considered "ethical" or "socially responsible." The question that we may naturally ask concerns whose interests these stakeholders really represent. Again, when it comes to corporate social responsibility, the narrow interests of particular groups are often dressed up as the cosmopolitan or universal aspirations of all peoples, and especially of the poor.

Debora Spar and David Yoffie of the Harvard Business School have suggested that firms will often self-regulate in the face of these strong societal and/or governmental pressures. Cases of self-regulation "are common," they argue, "more common by far than the race-to-the-bottom literature would suggest." Among the cases they cite are a 1981 agreement struck at the International Chamber of Commerce to harmonize environmental guidelines for MNEs; a 1984 safety and environmental program launched after the Bhopal chemical explosion in India by leading chemical companies, known as Responsible Care; a 1997 agreement by a group of leading textile firms accused of using "sweatshop" labor to form the Apparel Industry Partnership; and the SA8000 code established by a private group to monitor and certify social and labor practices among MNEs. They do not mention a similar nongovernmental effort, the Global Reporting Initiative, which calls on MNEs to provide "triple bottom-line" accounting in which environmental and labor data are presented alongside the company's balance sheet and income statement, thereby increasing transparency with respect to business practices in these areas.[34] In fact, an increasing number of companies are providing separate corporate social responsibility reports that describe their environmental and labor practices, as well as their community engagement.

Spar and Yoffie argue that self-regulation has several advantages over other types of international cooperation. First, it is probably quicker to achieve than an intergovernmental, multilateral agreement. Second, it enables firms to transfer the costs associated with any self-imposed regulatory policies onto their consumers. Third, it may enhance the reputations of the participating firms and win them valuable public relations space in the media. Finally, self-regulation may simply lead to more effective and efficient strategies for dealing with the problem at hand, since "politics" is kept to a minimum.[35]

Yet there are possible downsides associated with this approach that should be highlighted as well. Leaving aside the obvious problem of "contract" or regulatory enforcement, private-sector self-regulation poses the question, "in whose interest?" To be sure, exactly the same question can be asked with respect to state-led regulation. According to the "Chicago" or "Public Choice" school of economic theory, regulation is always designed in the interest of the regulated industry. In this model, industry "buys" regulation from government officials in return for some form of market protection. But rent-seeking can be mitigated in a competitive market environment because, as competition increases, regulators will face a more complex negotiating environment, with multiple interests to satisfy and, as a result, their preferred solution may be to level the playing field for all market participants. State-led regulation also emerges out of a more or less transparent political process, at least in the advanced industrial states, whereas the same cannot be said for private-sector agreements.

Further, private-sector self-regulation may reflect the demands of vocal special interest groups in the industrial world rather than that of host governments or, say, the poor in these countries. Let us suppose for the moment that FDI is a powerful instrument for poverty reduction.[36] If one were committed to that objective, it would then be perverse to place brakes on such investment, even if one had other cherished goals for FDI—or wanted to do away with FDI altogether. To put this in other words, those who call for greater "corporate social responsibility" have to recognize that higher performance standards may lead to trade-offs against other values.

In addition, self-regulation may serve to promote or enforce a form of cartelistic behavior on the part of multinational firms, in which these companies work together to drive out the competition. The setting of "high" environmental standards by an industry group, for example, may be a noble objective, but the costs associated with its realization may be affordable only for the largest MNEs. The executives of these firms thus wrap themselves in the cloak of corporate social responsibility while they use the new standards to help eliminate any competition they might face from small and medium-sized enterprises, which cannot pay the heavy costs associated with this wide array of social obligations. By inadvertently reducing competition and by raising the costs of doing business, corporate social responsibility may be welfare destroying for host countries, not to mention for entrepreneurs, who face ever-higher barriers to market entry.

Finally, the adoption of self-regulation and codes of conduct may lead to a moral hazard problem in which governments provide fewer public goods than they ought to in expectation of their provision by private-sector firms. Ruggie has stated the problem well: "corporate leaders have begun to recognize that the concept of corporate social responsibility . . . is infinitely elastic: the more they do, the more they will be asked to do. As a result, business leaders are beginning to ask, 'Where is the public sector?' "[37]

Self-regulation and corporate social responsibility, then, are unlikely to solve the problems of justice in investment. Indeed, they could worsen the problem by encouraging governments to evade their regulatory responsibilities while placing greater social burdens on companies that may be ill prepared to deal with them. If we seek international justice, then it is governments that must take the lead in structuring fair arrangements, for better or for worse.

Setting the Ethical Agenda for Multinationals: The United Nations Global Compact

But national governments, acting on their own, are often unable or unwilling to regulate multinational firms in a way that is compatible with the aspirations of at least some vocal members of "global" civil society. It was the belief that the normative gaps between governments, "civil society," and the private sector had to be closed in the interest of maintaining an open world economy and avoiding a globalization backlash that led the United Nations secretary general Kofi Annan to launch his Global Compact initiative at the 1999 World Economic Forum in Davos, Switzerland. There, "Annan called on business leaders to embrace a set of shared values and principles in the areas of human rights, labor standards, and environmental practices."[38] Table 5.1 spells out the Global Compact's nine basic principles.

According to the head of the United Nations Global Compact office, Georg Kell, the Compact was meant to contribute to "a more stable and socially just international economic order" by addressing many of the "negative phenomena associated with globalization." To the United Nations, these include rising inequality within and among nations, the increasing power of MNEs in the global economy, and the unleashing of a "race to the bottom in which corporations encourage the continuous reduction in labor and environmental standards and they seek to invest where standards are the lowest."[39] Clearly, it is not the United Nations' view that unregulated foreign direct investment can contribute to the creation of a just global economy. Instead, multinational firms must be harnessed to a normative framework that reflects the emerging set of "global" values.

The Global Compact thus invites companies to sign on to its nine broad principles of human rights, labor standards, and environmental practices—which are all drawn from existing United Nations declarations—thereby certifying themselves in a manner that is consistent with the normative preferences of United Nations member states. In this way, according to Ruggie, "Companies are encouraged to move toward 'good practices' as understood by the broader international community, rather than relying

TABLE 5.1
The U.N. Global Compact

Human Rights

Principle 1.   Businesses should support and respect the protection of internationally proclaimed human rights within their sphere of influence; and

Principle 2.   make sure that they are not complicit in human rights abuses.

Labor Standards

Principle 3.   Businesses should uphold the freedom of association and the effective recognition of the right to collective bargaining;

Principle 4.   the elimination of all forms of forced and compulsory labor;

Principle 5.   the effective abolition of child labor; and

Principle 6.   eliminate discrimination in respect of employment and occupation.

Environment

Principle 7.   Businesses should support a precautionary approach to environmental challenges;

Principle 8.   undertake initiatives to promote greater environmental responsibility; and

Principle 9.   encourage the development and diffusion of environmentally friendly technologies.

Source: U.N. Global Compact Office

on their often superior bargaining position vis-à-vis national authorities, especially in small and poor states, to get away with less."[40] The United Nations Global Compact office encourages member firms to promote partnerships with NGOs and the public sector and to present case studies that detail what firms are doing specifically to advance the Compact's principles.

But how widely accepted are the Global Compact's principles in fact? It is notable that Ruggie, one of the Compact's architects, stresses that it "is *not* a code of conduct. . . . In any event, the United Nations General Assembly could not generate a meaningful code of conduct at this time even if that were deemed desirable; the only countries eager to launch such an effort are equally unfriendly to the private sector, human rights, labor standards and the environment." In fact, he emphasizes that "many of the Global Compact's principles cannot be defined at this time with the precision required for a viable code of conduct."[41]

A few paragraphs later, however, he states that "the Compact is based on principles that were universally endorsed by governments, thus they stipulate the kind of global society to which the entire international community aspires."[42] But what kind of society is that? Clearly, there is no simple answer to that question. More accurately, the Compact operates at a vague enough level to be acceptable to United Nations members and to MNEs without holding any of these parties accountable for meeting a specific set of global operating standards. The Compact comes with no sanctions or enforcement mechanisms, and firms may have very different interpretations of what the Compact implies for their operations "on the ground."

That being said, the contribution of the Global Compact to contemporary normative discourse, if not yet corporate practice with respect to investment policy, should not be minimized. Today, hundreds of multinationals have joined the Global Compact and, in their annual reports, discuss their policies on human rights, labor standards, and the environment. That has promoted widespread debate about the multinational as a social actor, and has caused managers and institutional and individual shareholders to think more broadly about firms' responsibilities toward the governments and communities where they are based. Whether that debate will have a material outcome remains to be seen, but it has certainly heightened public awareness concerning many of the issues surrounding international economic justice, and particularly the relationship between the MNE and development.

Conclusions

I have argued in this chapter that justice in investment remains both elusive and necessary. It is elusive because of the "lumpy" nature of investment decisions, which motivates each party—government and multinational firm—to extract the most benefit over the project's lifetime. It is necessary because, without some conception of fairness, relations between host countries and firms will be prone to conflict, potentially undermining the role that investment can play in economic development. A critical step in the quest for justice in investment is therefore to lengthen the shadow of the future by nesting one-shot transactions into an "iterated game," for example by embedding particular investments in the context of bilateral and/or multilateral investment treaties. By viewing a particular investment decision as one that is part of a long-term flow of foreign capital, both states and firms may adjust their expectations, lifting their gaze from short-term profit maximization or rent seeking to mutually beneficial relationships in which investment serves as a motor for growth.

At the same time as investment treaties are proliferating, corporate codes of conduct and expressions of corporate social responsibility have also become commonplace. In the context of a global economy, international organizations have naturally stepped into this realm, with the OECD's aborted Multilateral Agreement on Investment and the United Nations' purposefully vague Global Compact providing the most prominent examples. These represent further attempts to provide international investment with a normative framework.

Excessive skepticism about this movement toward justice in investment would, I think, be unwarranted. From a historical perspective, the change in discourse between developing world governments and multinational enterprises has been dramatic over the past thirty or forty years. Not so long ago, multinational firms routinely faced the threat of expropriation by developing countries. In 1974, for example, several developing-country members of the United Nations lobbied "for the right to nationalize the assets of trans-national corporations in their territories and to freely determine the level of compensation shareholders would receive."[43] Today, there is a deep network of bilateral and multilateral investment treaties and dispute settlement procedures that provide frameworks for arbitrating and resolving differences between states and multinational firms.

To be sure, there is undoubtedly a pragmatic or realist element to this evolution. As Franck has written, "Fairness, in the law pertaining to foreign investments, is important not merely because it is a moral requisite, but because in its absence a major source of development capital would dry up, magnifying and perpetuating the unfairness of the existing inequalities between rich and poor. Thus a double imperative drives the search for a fairness consensus."[44]

Franck's double imperative is suggestive of the theory of economic justice we have presented in this book. I have argued that states pursue justice largely for self-interested reasons, in that fairness promotes the stability and robustness of given institutional arrangements. If governments and firms find that this pursuit leads to a more stable investment climate as well, then it has much to recommend it as a contributor to development policy.

6

TOWARD A LEVEL PLAYING FIELD:
A POLICY AGENDA

When politicians and experts become timid
about giving importance to moral commitments,
realism is absent.
—Gunnar Myrdal

Something like a normative revolution is now under way with respect to the global economy. Many critics—including some hard-boiled economists— have accused its underlying structures of being "unfair" or "unjust," especially to developing countries and to the poor within them. The continuing presence of millions of persons in poverty as we enter the twenty-first century, without access to the most basic goods and services that are necessary to preserve human life, much less dignity, naturally raises outcries from around the world and across the political spectrum that the international community must do better in the years ahead.

Few readers would disagree with that overall assessment. But how—and to whom—should we allocate scarce resources to meet the challenges posed by poverty and under-development? Should we strive for a global tax agency that redistributes wealth from rich to poor, from a Bill Gates (who already makes sizeable transfers to global health initiatives voluntarily) to the African smallholder?

Or do we focus instead on reforming existing institutions—such as the World Trade Organization (WTO)—in an effort to make them more responsive to growth and development objectives?

The main purpose of this concluding chapter is to discuss how the major international institutions seem to conceptualize the problem of economic justice in the world today and to map the contours of some politically feasible changes with respect to contemporary economic arrangements—that is, changes that can be viewed as broadly welfare-enhancing. As I will demonstrate, the current approach being taken to the problem of "global poverty" by institutions such as the World Bank powerfully reflects the growing influence of cosmopolitan sentiments and "poverty reduction" is now widely acclaimed as one of the international community's principal objectives. I will suggest some of the limitations associated with that policy framework, develop some alternatives, and then conclude with thoughts for future research, focusing on the need for developing and refining theories of institutional change.

Poverty Reduction as Economic Justice

In a year 2000 speech to his board of directors, the former World Bank president James Wolfensohn provided a litany of normative complaints about the state of the global economy. Among its moral failings, he emphasized that "*something is wrong* when 1.2. billion people still live on less than a dollar a day" (italics added). He urged the international community to shoulder its responsibilities toward these most vulnerable persons.

In recent years, the major multilateral institutions have been given a renewed mandate by their member states to attack global poverty, and the United Nations has formulated an ambitious set of Millennium Development Goals (MDGs) that include the objective of halving the number of people living on less than one dollar per day by the year 2015.[1] The World Bank now asserts that "poverty reduction is the most urgent task facing humanity today."[2] The WTO promises that "international trade can play a major role in economic development and the alleviation of poverty," and in 2001 it launched its "Doha Development Round" of trade negotiations.[3] More laconically, the International Monetary Fund (IMF) has reported that "the September 1999 Annual Meetings (of the World Bank and IMF) resulted in a clear mandate for the IMF to integrate the objectives of poverty reduction and growth more fully into its operations . . . and to base these operations on national poverty reduction strategies."[4] In short, the IMF is now expected by its member states to be "more pro-poor and more pro-growth."[5]

Although it is not possible here to provide a complete intellectual history of this "shift" toward a more "pro-poor" policy stance within the multilateral institutions, the role of nongovernmental organizations (NGOs) as normative transmission belts is one that has been highlighted by some scholars and it merits fuller discussion.[6] The Catholic Church, for example, played an important role in lobbying for developing-world debt reduction and relief during its Jubilee 2000 campaign, and organizations such as Oxfam have long argued that the trade regime has been insufficiently focused on the conditions of the poor. NGOs have gained increasing access to and voice at the

World Bank, where former president Wolfensohn was an articulate advocate of "pro-poor" development policies.

The intriguing possibility that NGOs have had some success in influencing the multilateral organizations and providing them with normative guidance is suggestive of constructivist theories of world politics. According to the constructivist logic, world politics is a contested social realm in which different actors vie for influence by defining the fundamental terms of debate. For example, realists view "anarchy" as the defining feature of the international system, and from that condition springs the insecurity, arms races, and wars that constitute so much of political history. Given that realist vision of how the world works, it follows that states have an "interest" in national security, which requires them to invest heavily in military power.

But anarchy does not seem to cast its warlike shadow when states are democratic. Democracies, being peace-loving, do not threaten other democratic regimes. How, then, do we conceptualize the relationship between anarchy and interests in this case? Is government type more significant than anarchy in shaping and explaining international relations? If so, then the anarchy condition does not define world politics in any absolute or objective manner. In the words of Alexander Wendt, "anarchy is what states make of it."[7]

Just as "anarchy is what states make of it" from the constructivist perspective, so too are problems of development. Traditionally, in explaining foreign economic policy, for example, political scientists have emphasized the role of special interest groups, such as oil companies, defense industries, or financial institutions. These groups have a strong material interest in open markets overseas, and as a consequence they are willing to expend the time and money needed to lobby politicians at home and abroad to win market access, especially in bigger foreign countries with the largest number of wealthy consumers.

But there is no reason to assume that only economic interest groups have political power in shaping the terms of normative debate over foreign policy. Representatives of civil society, including church groups, human rights organizations, and other NGOs, may also influence politicians, because they provide them with a moral framework or a set of normative ideas about how the world *ought* to work. These normative ideas can be useful to politicians as they seek to distinguish themselves from their rivals in winning electoral votes. Championing the rights of Catholics in China, for example, may be as politically valuable to a congressman in a heavily religious district in New Jersey as advocating textile quotas is to a politician in South Carolina.

The political scientists Martha Finnemore and Kathryn Sikkink have conducted groundbreaking research that highlights the role of these "norm entrepreneurs" in world politics. "Norm entrepreneurs" harness principled ideas to their political purpose, whether the objective is women's suffrage, human rights, or famine relief. They argue that norm entrepreneurs are playing a growing role on the international scene, as persons around the world become more sensitive to calls for human rights and social justice. With modern communications, people also become increasingly aware of material differences around the world, and as a result these differences become subject to moral inquiry. It is the role of norm entrepreneurs to exploit these material differences as a basis for political change, such as an increase in foreign aid spending or a renewed commitment by the multilateral development agencies to poverty reduction.[8]

To be sure, the "pro-poor" stance of the World Bank and the IMF could reflect other pressures beyond those of norm entrepreneurs (and the NGOs they influence). Since the attacks of September 2001, for example, some politicians and bureaucrats have drawn a connection between poverty and terrorism, suggesting that poverty reduction is in the security interest of states. In a more cynical vein, institutions such as the World Bank and the IMF may simply view "pro-poor" policies as being self-serving, providing them with fresh arguments for increases in their budgets and staffing. Still, whatever the ultimate cause for its political appeal, cosmopolitan theory as an approach to development policy—and particularly the view that "the poor" ought to be at the focal point of our international concerns—has undoubtedly become more prominent.

So let us then suppose that the model of international economic justice now being pursued by the major international financial institutions is one of targeting the poorest citizens in the poorest countries. Is this quasi-prioritarian approach deserving of our support?

The first question that we might raise as we explore this philosophy of poverty reduction concerns the site of the alleged injustice. Under the World Bank's model, it seems that there are two: first, national systems of welfare within developing countries, which have failed to make adequate transfers to their poorest citizens; second, the society of states, which has failed to meet its collective responsibility to the world's poor by filling the developing world's budgetary gap and meeting the poor's basic needs—hence the MDGs' demand for a significant increase in foreign aid spending. But why is it that the domestic social compact in most countries (both developing and industrial) fails to meet the needs of society's most vulnerable citizens? That is a question that has gone by the wayside, and instead poverty reduction is being treated fundamentally as an economic rather than a political problem—a problem that can be solved by additional resources.

By way of background, it will be useful to provide a sketch of this poverty-reduction approach to economic development. When poor countries come to the international financial institutions for economic assistance, they are now required to present "poverty reduction" strategies as a condition for fresh loans. Programs supported under this Poverty Reduction Growth Facility (PRGF) increase the amount of public spending beyond the amount that would normally be the case under typical IMF conditionality clauses, so long as such higher spending results in an increase in expenditures that are deemed to be "pro-poor." Working with the World Bank and bilateral donors, the IMF's hope is that the rise in public spending called for by a PRGF will be supported by foreign assistance, although the Fund now accepts the need for "higher spending . . . when a shortfall in assistance materializes."[9]

The particular public expenditures that are deemed pro-poor include education and health care. According to the Fund, "Countries with PRGF-supported programs are allocating more to education and health care, as a percent of GDP [gross domestic product], as a share of total government spending, and in per capita terms."[10] It should be emphasized, however, that the Fund admits that its capacity to monitor whether these additional expenditures are really pro-poor or not is in need of improvement, and this requires more sophisticated "poverty and social impact analysis." Additional education spending, for example, might benefit privileged bureaucrats rather than poor children.

But let us put aside that possibility and suppose that the PRGF is used efficiently and effectively. The underlying assumption of this policy framework must be that national welfare systems have failed only because they face a budget constraint that is inadequate to provide the "public goods" demanded by the citizenry, and especially by those who are poorest. Because government funds are simply inadequate to meet even the most basic social needs, the poor are denied access to services like health care. The international system therefore has the duty to provide the additional funds needed to alleviate this human suffering.

From a Rawlsian perspective on international economic justice, at least as articulated in *The Law of Peoples*, this general framework must be seen as fundamentally flawed. As noted in chapter 3, Rawls assumed that every well-ordered society would have the wherewithal to provide for the basic needs of all its citizens. If there is a failure to create a just society that takes cares of those who are least advantaged, it therefore reflects a political shortcoming as opposed to an economic one. The issue then is whether foreign country A has the duty, much less the capacity, to intervene in unjust society B in order to alleviate suffering.

Facing societies that are fundamentally unjust, Rawls would have likely expressed skepticism about the ability of outsiders to make a significant difference to the least advantaged in those countries, and he would probably have questioned whether there was even a moral obligation to act in this case. He would, however, have supported a limited "duty of assistance" that helps "burdened societies" achieve the political and social reforms needed in order to build just social compacts. Again, he would have placed the emphasis on domestic institutional reform as opposed to direct intervention to help "the poor."

The liberal internationalist would also take a different approach to poverty reduction. While undoubtedly agreeing with the ultimate objective, the liberal internationalist would emphasize the need for policies among states that promote the economic growth of each one; in short, policies that are welfare-enhancing for all. Liberal internationalists would certainly support increased foreign aid, but with a focus on helping poor *countries* escape poverty, chiefly by building up their capacity to join the global economy. In contrast, they would recognize that countries may take very different approaches to domestic poverty reduction, with some focusing on increasing opportunities for the poor, while others emphasize direct income transfers.

The liberal internationalist would also emphasize that granting foreign aid to developing countries without opening industrial world markets to their exports is like giving a child a scholarship to Harvard or Oxford, but then denying the student a job upon graduation because of his or her race or gender. It follows that the emphasis on "pro-poor" aid in the presence of industrial world protectionism provides a shining example of great-power hypocrisy. It also severely undermines aid's effectiveness, and in so doing reduces domestic political support for that particular use of tax revenues. Reform of the trade regime in a way that promotes market access, therefore, would be a priority of the liberal internationalist, and pointing out the shameful nature of industrial-world protectionism would motivate many a jeremiad.

Given the fact that protectionism limits the efficacy of pro-poor policies, what then explains their widespread political attraction? As already noted, cosmopolitan theory could be responding both to lofty normative concerns and to the nitty-gritty political demands of activists in nongovernmental organizations, and indeed it is this particular mix that may make it such a tempting concoction. Since the end of the Cold War, there has been a renewed emphasis around the world on human rights, and that provides cosmopolitan theory, and the pro-poor policies it reflects with some of its contemporary resonance. Religious groups and many other NGOs have been quick to place these sentiments at the heart of their political campaigns and their lobbying of international institutions, and a number of politicians and bureaucrats have responded by recognizing the value of this normative framework in terms of their own particular interests. As a consequence, the elimination of global poverty has risen to the top of the international community's economic agenda.

At the same time, pro-poor foreign aid policies can hardly substitute for higher levels of trade and investment, which are the global economy's most powerful contributors to growth. But reform of the trade regime requires giving developing-world governments substantially more voice than they have at present in the negotiating process, and as we have seen, that would require revisiting the norm of strict reciprocity that heavily influences trade talks. Pro-poor policies may or may not be effective—the jury is still out—but they are certainly not sufficient.

Reforming the International Regimes

The normative theory presented in this book has sought not only to illuminate the shortcomings of the contempo-

rary economic order, but also to point the way toward politically feasible reform and change. By politically feasible
I do not mean, of course, that states will pass a particular
law tomorrow or the next day, or that the major multilateral organizations will reform their decision-making
structures over the short run. What I mean, instead, is that
the reforms I am suggesting are supposed to be explicitly
welfare-enhancing rather than welfare-reducing, and so
they should escape at least one fundamental objection that
self-interested governments might put before them.

In considering the possibility of reform within the sub-
stantive issue areas I have treated in this book, it may be
useful to provide a basic matrix diagram that compares
the actual set of arrangements for trade, aid, migration,
labor, and investment with what the politically feasible
alternative, the "realistic utopia," might look like. That
matrix appears as table 6.1.

As this matrix suggests, each arrangement or regime has
its strengths and weaknesses from a normative perspective. To be sure, trade, aid, and investment are all unam-
biguously welfare-enhancing (although there is certainly
some contestation concerning aid in this respect), and undoubtedly that is why these instruments hold widespread
appeal for the international community. But each of them
has fundamental gaps in their structure that should be addressed. Let us briefly discuss each regime in turn.

With respect to the trade regime, the fundamental normative problem we have uncovered is the principle of
strict reciprocity that drives trade negotiations. Since
trade negotiators come to the multilateral talks with limited stores of political capital, they focus on making big
deals among big countries, in tit-for-tat fashion. This
leaves small developing countries on the margins, with

TABLE 6.1
Judging the Global Economy

	Trade	Aid	Migration	Labor	Investment
Inclusive	Yes (WTO)	Yes (World Bank)	No, there is no multilateral regime	Yes (ILO)	No, there is no multilateral regime; most investment treaties are bilateral
Participatory	Partially, but limited by principle of strict reciprocity	Partially, but aid decisions are driven by industrial countries	No, immigration decisions are usually made unilaterally by states	Yes	Partially, but MAI was negotiated mainly among industrial nations, with little input from developing countries
Welfare-enhancing	Yes, but more liberalization is needed	Yes, but more aid should be directed to trade-capacity building	Yes, for receiving state; contested for sender	Contested: states disagree about relationship between higher labor standards and growth	Yes, but need to limit investment subsidies

Source: Author

little influence over the proceedings. As a consequence, they have been unable to extract many concessions with respect to the areas of greatest importance to them, such as agriculture.

I have already argued that the principle of strict reciprocity should be replaced by a principle of diffuse reciprocity, or what trade negotiators call relaxed reciprocity. This does not mean that any state should be allowed to escape its obligations under the multilateral trade agreements—as "special and differential" status has allowed developing countries to do—but instead the negotiations should be modified to incorporate developing-world concerns while still holding them responsible for meeting certain trade liberalization measures.

As noted in chapter 2, it does appear that this principle of diffuse reciprocity has played a role, if only a small one, in the actual context of the postwar trade negotiations. That is, the outcomes of these talks are not easily explained solely by reference to the distribution of economic or military power. A "residual" of concessions has been left over that appear to reflect a concern with achieving agreements that all parties agree are fair or of mutual advantage. To be sure, the international community can do much more, but the effort that has been undertaken speaks to the broadest argument of this book: that justice and fairness matter to global economic arrangements.

Although there is no formal aid regime as such—most aid decisions are taken within national aid agencies in the major industrial nations—the priorities of the World Bank and the IMF may be said to reflect the broader normative concerns of the aid community at any given time, and of course they are significant providers of funds in their own right. These institutions are broadly inclusive, but participation in their decision making is limited; in the IMF, for example, decisions often reflect the power of its biggest shareholders. And within national aid agencies, of course, domestic politics loom large, with little voice given to developing countries. Reforming the multilateral lending agencies in a way that gives recipient governments greater voice would seem a major step forward for the cause of international economic justice, while still respecting the rights of the most powerful shareholders, whose taxpayers, after all, provide much of their working capital.

Aid should also be focused more directly on trade capacity building. As already stated, it does little good to provide countries with aid if they cannot increase their exports; that is the definition of absurdity. But developing countries are constrained from taking advantage of trading opportunities in many ways, and the international community has an interest in justice in helping them overcome these barriers.

Turning to migration and labor, these cases present in some ways the most difficult topics for a theory of international economic justice. That is not surprising, for in no realm do considerations of human rights loom so large, and pitting those rights against other values naturally raises troubling questions of justice and fairness. As we have seen, there is no umbrella regime covering migration, and the relevant policies are mainly decided unilaterally by nation-states. That means that there is ample scope for creating a more inclusive, participatory, and welfare-enhancing migration regime. I have already argued that one good place to launch welfare-enhancing multilateral discussions would be around the topic of worker remittances, with the objective of lowering the high fees that workers pay in order to transfer their funds home.

Paradoxically, the labor regime—as exemplified by the International Labor Organization (ILO)—is perhaps the most inclusive and participatory of all the arrangements we have considered, but perhaps also the most contested in terms of its welfare-enhancing qualities. This is because states continue to debate the precise meaning of the core labor standards that they have agreed on—for example, the abolition of child labor and the right to association and collective bargaining—and they question the relationship between applying these standards and their own growth prospects. Developing countries, in particular, are fearful that the industrial nations seeks to link these standards to trade agreements for self-serving, protectionist reasons rather than out of any concern for workers. I have argued that the call for higher labor standards is consistent with a more just global economy to the extent that it is tied to a comprehensive development strategy, one that increases productivity and growth in the developing-world. In contrast, demanding higher standards without taking responsibility for helping to pay for them or nest them in a broader development framework is the essence of "cheap talk."

In recent years, foreign direct investment has become increasingly important to the growth prospects of developing countries—a dramatic turnabout, given that not so many years ago many of these same countries frowned on such investment. The relationship between developing-world governments and multinational enterprises, however, is fraught with tension, particularly in the context of bargains that each side may be tempted to view as "one-shot." Indeed, even the industrial countries have competed desperately among themselves to attract these investment dollars, providing rich subsidies that will never be repaid through tax revenues. The investment "regime," to the extent that one exists, points powerfully to the prisoner's dilemma logic that still shapes the global economy in important respects and that favors only the richest nations. Still, it is interesting that this topic has been taken up both within nations—such as the United States—and among them, for example within the context of the Organization for Economic Cooperation and Development. Overcoming the prisoner's dilemma with respect to investment subsidies would mark a major step forward in leveling the global playing field.

Economic Justice and Political Change

How can we move forward in building a progressive, policy-relevant research agenda with respect to international economic justice? I believe that we must give renewed attention to the classic problems of political reform and change. When we design and build our social institutions, ensuring stability and preservation of a given status quo are usually the chief characteristics that we seek. The institutions that we create "fix" our social arrangements, for better or for worse. Once established, these institutions follow a "path-dependent" course; they are "sticky" and difficult, by design, to change.

Yet peaceful change does come to our institutions, and providing a theory of how it occurs remains one of the central challenges facing contemporary social science. As Samuel Huntington has written, "Revolutions are rare. Reform, perhaps, is even rarer. . . . The way of the reformer is hard."[11] Unlike the revolutionary, the reformer must seek to convince entrenched interests that peaceful change is in his or her best interest. A broad coalition for change must be built, with all the political difficulties that such coalition building entails.

When it comes to the pursuit of a fairer world economy, the prospect of change is especially daunting. Albert Hirschman once defined policy reform as a change in which "the power of hitherto privileged groups is curbed and the economic position and social status of underprivileged groups is correspondingly improved." For Huntington, reform "means a change in the direction of greater social, economic, or political equality."[12] Although we have many case studies of political and economic change, modern social science is still struggling to develop broad covering theories and models of the important social reforms that have taken place, which have moved in the direction of greater opportunity. Applying any theories that we develop to the international level poses additional difficulties, given the absence of an authoritative decision maker.

Without theories of reform and change, it is very difficult to provide compelling advice to public officials about how to make the world a better place. There is no shortage of ideas for improving the economic prospects of nations and persons that could be put on the policy agenda, but how to put them into effect is the real question we must answer. Absent compelling theories of change, we are sometimes left to *assume* that the desired reforms will simply occur, as if by an invisible hand. The good news is that problems of change are now becoming prominent on the agenda of modern political economy.

The problem of political and institutional change is relevant to every level of analysis in the study of economic justice. At the international level, take the case of the

WTO and its reciprocity-based bargaining structure. Although tit-for-tat reciprocity has undoubtedly promoted market access liberalization between the United States and the European Union, we have argued that it has not responded to the needs of developing countries in important respects, for example by failing to generate greater market opening in agriculture. As a result, developing countries cannot export as much as they would like in the very sector where many of them hold comparative advantage, undermining the very purpose of a free trade regime.

How do we change the basic structure of the WTO in a way that promotes the economic interests of all its members and transforms it into a system of mutual advantage? From a realist perspective, that question may only be answered as developing countries gradually increase their market and military power, threatening the status quo if changes are not made. At the same time, we should recognize that a positive attribute of the trade regime is that it permits new powers to exercise their influence in the multilateral framework; it is not an exclusive club barring entry to states that become more powerful by their own efforts. But impetus for reform of the WTO and other international institutions could also come from within the industrial countries themselves, as new coalitions of political actors coalesce around issues of economic development and poverty reduction.

At the domestic level, take the case of social safety nets and other distributive policies. Policy makers and academics from the industrial world have often urged developing countries to knit tighter safety nets for their citizens as they open their economies to world trade. But these calls usually go unheeded, simply because they imply changes in income distribution that are impossible to achieve within many domestic polities, where fiscal policy is weak or ineffective. We know that some countries *have* managed successfully to redistribute income over time—just think of the European welfare states—but we lack broad *theories* about *how* these governments have managed to do so that can help us to inform developing-world leaders as they engage in policy reform. This absence of theory about policy change should make us appropriately modest when it comes to giving normative advice.

Efforts to move the international economy in the direction of greater fairness must therefore prove difficult, in the face of domestic political structures that reward certain groups over others, and in the face of international politics in which the distribution of wealth and power still matters greatly to outcomes. Institutional stickiness remains the rule, and at both the international and domestic levels there is a great deal of unfairness built into the policies that actually exist.

Still, changes do occur, as new ideas and norms of behavior meet up with receptive political audiences. Today, many ideas concerning international economic justice are being floated, and many political groups are seeking to promote the cause of economic development. There are already some signs that these ideas and interests are making a difference with respect to the leading international economic institutions, if ever so slightly. For all we know, the seeds of change have already been planted, waiting to sprout new approaches to the world's most pressing problems.

If we are to give careful consideration to alternative schemes for meeting the needs of development and poverty reduction, it follows that we must improve our ability to match different theories of distributive justice with the available economic models and data. Whether our concern is primarily with our own nation's welfare in the presence of greater openness, or with the fate of the global poor, we should seek to learn more about how globalization is, in practice, influencing the variables that concern us, such as poverty or income inequality. That exercise also has important policy implications. If we find, for example, that greater openness is leading to reduced levels of world poverty, then those of us who care about that variable should probably advocate more globalization rather than less.

In this book I have tried to contribute to the emerging debate over the international economy's normative underpinnings. I have argued that in a community of sovereign states, economic justice must be conceived of as an arrangement of mutual advantage, one that is welfare-enhancing for all. Given the uncertainties associated with the future course of world politics, the search for justice, for a leveler playing field, will be driven primarily by a self-interested desire on the part of governments to avoid conflict and instability in their exchange relationships.

To be sure, the theory of justice presented here is, perhaps paradoxically, heavily statist and market-oriented in its orientation, and many readers—particularly those of cosmopolitan sentiment—may be disappointed that I have not addressed more directly the plight of the world's least-advantaged persons, or given more weight to the role of NGOs and multinational firms. I would only respond that if our shared concern is with those who are least advantaged, then we must create an economic environment that promotes every state's opportunity to exercise its comparative advantage and enter the global economy. In the absence of such an environment, the challenge of poverty reduction will prove all the more intractable. As Kenneth

Boulding once wrote, "the nineteenth century, by failing to evolve an ethical ideology which could sustain it, produced the discontents which destroyed it."[13] As we enter the twenty-first century, the international community must strive to avoid a similar fate.

NOTES

PREFACE

The epigraph to this preface is cited in Sidney Fine, *Laissez-Faire and the General Welfare State* (Ann Arbor: University of Michigan Press, 1964), p. 177.

1. The most compelling statement of this position remains Charles Beitz, *Political Theory and International Relations* (Princeton, NJ: Princeton University Press, 1979).

2. Anthony Trollope, *The Way We Live Now* (1875; reprinted, New York: Modern Library, 2001), p. 323.

3. I thank James Caporaso for emphasizing this point.

4. Ronald Dworkin, *Sovereign Virtue* (Cambridge, MA: Harvard University Press, 2000).

CHAPTER ONE
ECONOMIC JUSTICE IN AN UNFAIR WORLD

Epigraph is from E. H. Carr, *The Twenty Years' Crisis* (1939; reprinted, New York: Harper and Row, 1962), p. 146.

1. Edward Gresser, "Toughest on the Poor," *Foreign Affairs*, November/December 2002, p. 9.

2. Elizabeth Becker, "Bush Aide Threatens to Sue EU," *International Herald Tribune*, 10 January 2003, p. 11.

3. Guy Verhofstadt, "Towards Ethical Globalization," *OECD Observer* 231/232 (May 2002): 4.

4. Joseph Stiglitz, "A Fair Deal for the World," *New York Review of Books*, 23 May 2002, p. 24.

5. I thank Michael Barnett for emphasizing this point. See United Nations Development Program, *Globalization with a Human Face* (New York: Oxford University Press, 1999);

United Nations Millennium Project, *Investing in Development: A Practical Plan to Achieve the Millennium Development Goals* (New York: United Nations, Millennium Project, 2005).

6. President George W. Bush, cited at www.whitehouse.gov/infocus/internationaltrade.

7. Derek Parfit, "Equality and Priority," *Ratio* 10, no. 3 (December 1997): 202–221.

8. For a review of the literature, see E. S. Phelps, *Economic Justice* (Baltimore: Penguin, 1973).

9. Thomas Schelling, *Choice and Consequences* (Cambridge, MA: Harvard University Press, 1984), p. 17.

10. Ronald Dworkin, *Sovereign Virtue* (Cambridge, MA: Harvard University Press, 2000), p. 6.

11. Hal Varian, "Distributive Justice, Welfare Economics and the Theory of Fairness," *Philosophy and Public Affairs* 4 (Spring 1975): 244.

12. Robert Nozick, *Anarchy, State and Utopia* (New York: Basic Books, 1974).

13. Notable examples include Charles Beitz, *Political Theory and International Relations* (Princeton, NJ: Princeton University Press, 1979); John Rawls, *The Law of Peoples* (Cambridge, MA: Harvard University Press, 1999); Thomas Pogge, ed., *Global Justice* (Oxford: Blackwell, 2001); and Peter Singer, *One World: The Ethics of Globalization* (New Haven, CT: Yale University Press, 2002).

14. Stanley Hoffmann, *Duties beyond Borders* (Syracuse, NY: Syracuse University Press, 1981), p. 141.

15. John Ruggie, "International Regimes, Transactions, and Change: Embedded Liberalism in the Postwar Economic Order," in *International Regimes*, ed. Stephen D. Krasner (Ithaca, NY: Cornell University Press, 1983).

16. See, e.g., William Cline, *Trade and Income Distribution* (Washington, DC: Institute for International Economics, 1997).

17. Dani Rodrik, *Has Globalization Gone Too Far?* (Washington, DC: Institute for International Economics, 1997), p. 1.

18. William Cline, *Trade and Income Distribution*, p. 275.

19. For an elaboration of this point, see Ethan B. Kapstein, *Sharing the Wealth: Workers and the World Economy* (New York: W. W. Norton, 1999).

20. Branko Milanovic, "True World Income Distribution, 1988 and 1993: First Calculation Based on Household Surveys Alone" (manuscript, World Bank, Development Research Group, 2000).

21. Thomas Pogge, "Cosmopolitanism and Sovereignty," *Ethics* 103 (October 1992): 48–49.

22. Parfit, "Equality and Priority."

23. Thomas W. Pogge, "Moral Universalism and Global Economic Justice," *Politics, Philosophy and Economics* 1 (February 2002): 43.

24. On these points, see Singer, *One World*.

25. Ethan Nadelmann, "Global Prohibition Regimes: The Evolution of Norms in International Society," *International Organization* 44, no. 4 (Autumn 1990): 483.

26. This point is developed by Martha Finnemore, *National Interests in International Society* (Ithaca, NY: Cornell University Press, 1996).

27. See the Web sites of these organizations: www.oxfam.org and www.savethechildren.org.uk.

28. Milanovic, "True World Income Distribution, 1988 and 1993."

29. Thomas Pogge, "An Egalitarian Law of Peoples," *Philosophy & Public Affairs* 23, no. 3 (Summer 1994): 220.

30. Christian Barry, "Global Justice: Aims, Arrangements, and Responsibilities," in *Can Institutions Have Duties?* ed. Toni Erskine (London: Palgrave, 2003), p. 226.

31. See Charles Beitz, "International Liberalism and Distributive Justice: A Survey of Recent Thought," *World Politics* 51 (January 1999): 269–296.

32. *Charles P. Kindleberger, American Business Abroad* (New Haven, CT: Yale University Press, 1969), p. 207.

33. I thank Branko Milanovic for the sports example.

34. An alternative label might be *institutional cosmopolitanism*, as developed by Thomas Pogge. See Pogge, "Cosmopolitanism and Sovereignty." The reason I do not adopt this term is because my emphasis in this book is on relations among state actors, and I distinguish that approach from a particular variant of cosmopolitan thought, namely prioritarianism.

35. For a classic statement and critique of hegemonic stability theory, see Robert Keohane, *After Hegemony: Cooperation and Discord in the World Political Economy* (Princeton, NJ: Princeton University Press, 1984).

36. Dani Rodrik, "Feasible Globalizations" (NBER Working Paper; W9129, August 2002), p. 24.

37. See, for example, Keohane, *After Hegemony.*

38. Beitz, *Political Theory.* I should emphasize that Beitz would probably not apply the liberal internationalist label to his work.

39. It is notable that Rawls himself would reject Beitz's application of his theory of justice to the international system; see Rawls, *Law of Peoples.*

40. Beitz, *Political Theory*, p. 142.

41. I thank Anne Krueger for highlighting this point.

42. Lawrence Summers, "Statement to the Development Committee of the World Bank and the International Monetary Fund" (17 April 2000, at www.imf.org/external/spring/2000/dc/usa.htm).

43. For an alternative view, see Mathias Risse, "Do We Live in an Unjust World?" (*Faculty Research Working Papers* RWP03–

049, Kennedy School of Government, Harvard University, December 2003).

44. The phrase is Francis Fukuyama's. See his *The End of History and the Last Man* (New York: Basic Books, 1992).

45. John Stuart Mill, *Principles of Political Economy* (1848; reprinted, New York: Penguin, 1978), p. 350.

46. Ruggie, "International Regimes."

47. Rawls, *Law of Peoples.*

48. I thank an anonymous reviewer for forcing me to address this point.

49. Pogge, "Egalitarian Law of Peoples," p. 217.

50. See Bruce Bueno de Mesquita and David Lalman, *War and Reason* (New Haven, CT: Yale University Press, 1992), p. 12.

51. For an elaboration of the model, see Jack Hirshleifer, *The Dark Side of the Force* (New York: Cambridge University Press, 2001).

52. Dale Copeland, "Economic Interdependence and War: A Theory of Trade Expectation," *International Security* 20, no. 4 (Spring 1996): 5–41.

53. Robert Keohane, "Reciprocity in International Relations," *International Organization* 40, 1 (Winter 1986): 27.

54. Ibid., p, 4.

55. Ibid., p. 10.

56. Ibid., p. 4.

57. Cited in Keohane, *After Hegemony*, p. 129.

58. Ibid.

59. Monica D. Blumenthal, et al., *More about Justifying Violence: Methodological Studies of Attitudes and Behavior* (Ann Arbor, MI: Institute for Social Research, University of Michigan, 1975), p. 108.

60. Donald J. Puchala and Raymond F. Hopkins, "International Regimes: Lessons from Inductive Analysis," in *Interna-*

tional Regimes, ed. Stephen D. Krasner (Ithaca, NY: Cornell University Press, 1983), p. 66.

61. I thank an anonymous reviewer for highlighting this point.

62. Francesco Parisi and Nita Ghei, "The Role of Reciprocity in International Law" (manuscript, George Mason University School of Law, n.d.), p. 24.

63. Keohane, "Reciprocity in International Relations," p. 8.

64. See, for example, the arguments in Scott Sagan, "Realist Perspectives on Ethical Norms" (manuscript, Stanford University, 2004).

65. Cited in Joel Rosenthal, "What the Sages Say" (lecture delivered at the Fletcher School of Law and Diplomacy, Tufts University, during the academic year 2000–2001, at www.cceia.org/printerfriendlymedia.php).

66. Andrew Hurrell, "Power, Institutions, and the Production of Inequality," in *Power in Global Governance*, ed. Michael Barnett and Raymond Duvall (New York: Cambridge University Press, 2005).

67. Carr, *Twenty Years Crisis*, p. 169.

68. I thank Michael Barnett for emphasizing this point.

69. For further elaboration of the concept of focal points, see Thomas Schelling, *The Strategy of Conflict* (Cambridge, MA: Harvard University Press, 1960). Whether or not uncertainty promotes cooperation remains disputed in the literature; there are strands in bargaining theory, for example, that suggest that uncertainty promotes conflict. See Robert Powell, "Bargaining Theory and International Conflict" (manuscript, University of California, Berkeley, 2004).

70. Barbara Koremenos, Charles Lipson, and Duncan Snidal, "The Rational Design of International Institutions," *International Organization* 55, no. 1 (Autumn 2001): 778.

71. Martin A. Nowak, Karen M. Page, and Karl Sigmund, "Fairness versus Reason in the Ultimatum Game," *Science*, 8 September 2000, p. 1773.

72. Ernst Fehr and Simon Gachter, "Fairness and Retaliation: The Economics of Reciprocity," *Journal of Economic Perspectives* 14, no. 3 (Summer 2000): 159–181.

73. Gary Bolton, et. al., "Testing Theories of Other-Regarding Behavior: A Sequence of Four Laboratory Studies" (manuscript, n.d.).

74. Keohane, "Reciprocity in International Relations," p. 23.

75. John Rawls, *A Theory of Justice* (Cambridge, MA: Harvard University Press, 1971), pp. 102–103.

76. Amanda Dickins, "Just Distributions: Economic Globalisation and International Distributive Justice" (paper presented at the annual meeting of the American Political Science Association, Boston, MA, August 2002), p. 12.

77. David Lewis, *Convention: A Philosophical Study* (Cambridge, MA: Harvard University Press, 1969).

78. It is David Hume who took the position that justice could be conceived of as a cooperative convention. He wrote that justice "may be properly called a convention or agreement betwixt us . . . since the actions of each of us have a reference to those of the other and are performed upon the supposition that something is to be performed on the other part. . . . [T]his experience assures us . . . that the sense of interest has become common to all our fellows and gives us a confidence of the future regularity of their conduct; and it is only on the expectation of this that our moderation and abstinence are founded." Cited in Dickins, "Just Distributions," p. 12.

79. Robert Axelrod, *The Evolution of Cooperation* (New York: Basic Books, 1984).

80. See Avner Greif, "Contract Enforceability and Economic Institutions in Early Trade: The Maghribi Traders' Coalition," *American Economic Review* 83, no. 3 (1993): 525–548.

81. Charles I. Jones, *Introduction to Economic Growth* (New York: Norton, 1998), p. 56.

82. Richard E. Baldwin, Henrik Braconier, and Rikard Forslid, "Multinationals, Endogenous Growth and Technological Spillovers: Theory and Evidence" (manuscript, August 1999), p. 2.

83. John E. Roemer, *Equality of Opportunity* (Cambridge, MA: Harvard University Press, 1998).

84. Humberto G. Llavador and John E. Roemer, "An Equal-Opportunity Approach to the Allocation of International Aid," *Journal of Development Economics* 64 (2001): 147–171.

85. It is interesting to note that, historically, governments appear to have acted with two minds when it comes to their own moral standing in world politics. After World War I, for example, the victorious allies imposed heavy war reparations on Germany, and it was made clear that Germany was responsible for the damage inflicted. At the same time, Article 227 of the Versailles Treaty stated that "the Allied and Associated Powers publicly arraign William II of Hohenzollern, formerly German Emperor, for a supreme offence against *international morality* and the sanctity of treaties" (italics added). After World War II, in contrast, Germany as a state was exonerated of wrongdoing, while individual Nazis were tried for their "crimes against humanity," and the infamous defense that "I was only serving my country" was found inexcusable by the court's judges. Today, an international criminal court hears cases of crimes against humanity carried out by individuals such as the former Serbian leader Slobodan Milosevic. Still, even though Germany was never implicated in any crime, the state did agree to pay restitution to Holocaust victims. Similarly, Switzerland created a fund for Holocaust victims whose bank accounts were seized during the war. In fact, a growing number of states or governments have claimed moral responsibility for their past actions in recent years, indicating a heightened awareness of moral issues

in world politics. On these issues, see Elazar Barkan, *The Guilt of Nations* (Baltimore: Johns Hopkins University Press, 2001).

86. Hedley Bull, *The Anarchical Society* (New York: Columbia University Press, 1977), p. 78.

CHAPTER TWO
FAIRNESS IN TRADE

Epigraph is from Alan Greenspan, "Globalization" (remarks to the Institute for International Economics, 2001).

1. Oxfam, *Rigged Rules and Double Standards: Trade, Globalization and the Fight against Poverty* (Oxford: Oxfam, 2002), p. 5.

2. Dani Rodrik, "Feasible Globalizations" (manuscript, Kennedy School of Government, 2002), p. 24.

3. See, for example, Edward Mansfield, *Power, Trade, and War* (Princeton, NJ: Princeton University Press, 1994).

4. Kenneth E. Boulding, "Defense and Opulence: The Ethics of International Economics," *American Economic Review* 41, no. 2 (May 1951): 217.

5. James Meade, *The Theory of International Economic Policy, Trade and Welfare* (New York: Oxford University Press, 1955).

6. Cited in Daniel Hausman and Michael McPherson, *Economic Analysis and Moral Philosophy* (New York: Cambridge University Press, 1996), p. 95.

7. Roger Howe and John Roemer, "Rawlsian Justice as the Core of a Game," *American Economic Review* 71 (December 1981): 880.

8. William Baumol, *Superfairness* (Cambridge, MA: MIT Press, 1988).

9. Paul Krugman and Maurice Obstfeld, *International Economics* (Reading, MA: Addison-Wesley, 2000), p. 224.

10. J. David Richardson, *Understanding International Trade* (Boston: Little, Brown, 1980).

11. Paul Samuelson, "International Trade and the Equalization of Factor Prices," *Economic Journal* 58 (June 1948): 163–183.

12. David Dollar and Aart Kraay, "Trade, Growth and Poverty" (World Bank Policy Research Working Papers no. 2615, 1 June 2001).

13. Charles Beitz, *Political Theory and International Relations* (Princeton, NJ: Princeton University Press, 1979), pp. 145–146.

14. Jagdish Bhagwati, "Free Trade: Why the AFL-CIO, the Sierra Club, and Congressman Gephardt Should Like It" (remarks presented on receiving the Seidman Award in Political Economy, 18 September 1998), p. 11.

15. Richardson, *Understanding International Trade*, p. 483.

16. Paul Krugman, "A Model of Innovation, Technology Transfer, and the World Distribution of Income," *Journal of Political Economy* 87 (April 1979):, 253–266.

17. Ibid., p. 261.

18. Daron Acemoglu and Jaume Ventura, "The World Income Distribution" (NBER Working Paper 8083, 2001), p. 2.

19. Paul Samuelson, "International Factor Price Equalization Once Again," *Economic Journal* 59 (June 1949): 181–197.

20. Robert D. Putnam, "Diplomacy and Domestic Politics: The Logic of Two-Level Games," *International Organization* 42, no. 3 (Summer 1988): 427–460.

21. For an exception, see Cecilia Albin, *Justice and Fairness in International Negotiation* (New York: Cambridge University Press, 2001).

22. Ibid., p. 105.

23. H. W. Arndt, *Essays in International Economics, 1944–1994* (Aldershot, UK: Avebury, 1995), p. 302.

24. Kenneth S. Chan, "The International Negotiation Game: Some Evidence From the Tokyo Round," *Review of Economics and Statistics* 67, no. 3 (August 1985): 463.

25. Ibid.

26. Cited in ibid., p. 464.

27. J. Michael Finger, Ulrich Reincke, and Adriana Castro, "Market Access Bargaining in the Uruguay Round: Rigid or Relaxed Reciprocity?" (World Bank Working Paper no. 2258, 1999), p. 7.

28. Neil McCulloch, L. Alan Winters, and Xavier Cirera, *Trade Liberalization and Poverty: A Handbook* (London: Centre for Economic Policy Research, 2001), p. 168.

29. Glenn W. Harrison, Thomas F. Rutherford, and David G. Tarr, "Quantifying the Uruguay Round," in *The Uruguay Round and Developing Countries*, ed. Will Martin and L. Alan Winters (Washington, DC: World Bank, 1995), p. 242.

30. Cited in Anne Krueger, *Trade Policy and Developing Nations* (Washington, DC: Brookings Institution, 1995), p. 45.

31. Hesham Youssef, *Special and Differential Treatment for Developing Countries in the WTO* (Geneva: South Centre, p. 5. n.d.), posted at www.southcentre.org/publications/s&d/toc.htm.

32. Stephen D. Krasner, *Structural Conflict* (Berkeley and Los Angeles: University of California Press, 1985).

33. T. N. Srinivasan, "Trade and Development: Developing Countries in the World Trading System: 1947–1999" (manuscript, Yale University, May 1999).

34. Cited in T. N. Srinivasan, *Developing Countries and the Multilateral Trading System* (Boulder, CO: Westview Press, 1998), p. 21.

35. John P. Lewis, "Oil, Other Scarcities, and the Poor Countries," *World Politics* 27 (1974): 66.

36. See Nigel Grimwade, *International Trade Policy: A Contemporary Analysis* (New York: Routledge, 1996), pp. 152–153.

37. Gerald M. Meier, *International Trade and Development* (New York: Harper and Row, 1963), pp. 175ff.

38. Srinivasan, *Developing Countries and the Multilateral Trading System*, p. 23.

39. Arndt, *Essays in International Economics*, p. 78.

40. Krueger, *Trade Policies and Developing Nations*, p. 40.

41. Robert Hudec, *Developing Countries in the GATT Legal System* (London: Trade Policy Research Centre, 1987).

42. For a useful background paper on this issue, see John R. Thomas, "HIV/AIDS Drugs, Patents, and the TRIPS Agreement: Issues and Options," in *CRS Report for Congress* (Washington, DC: Library of Congress, 27 July 2001); the citation is to p. 15.

43. Nicholas Eberstadt, "The Future of AIDS," *Foreign Affairs*, November/December 2002: p. 23.

44. For Oxfam's position, see chapter 8 of *Rigged Rules and Double Standards*.

45. I thank an anonymous reviewer for highlighting these questions.

46. Paul G. Harris and Patricia Siplon, "International Obligation and Human Health: Evolving Policy Responses to HIV/AIDS," *Ethics and International Affairs* 15, no. 2 (2001): 45.

47. See Ruth Levine, *Millions Saved: Proven Successes in Global Health* (Washington, DC: Center for Global Development, November 2004), p. 4.

48. Ravi Kanbur, "Development Economics and the Compensation Principle" (manuscript, Cornell University, June 2002), p. 1.

49. Harrison, Rutherford, and Tarr, "Quantifying the Uruguay Round," p. 242.

50. John Stuart Mill cited in Douglas Irwin, *Against the Tide: An Intellectual History of Free Trade* (Princeton, NJ: Princeton University Press, 1996), p. 183.

51. Richard Brecher and Ehsan Choudhri, "Pareto Gains from Trade Reconsidered: Compensating for Jobs Lost," *Journal of International Economics* 36, no. 3 (1994): 223–238.

CHAPTER THREE
ALLOCATING AID

1. John Rawls, *The Law of Peoples* (Cambridge, MA: Harvard University Press, 1999).

2. United Nations Millennium Project, *Investing in Development: A Practical Plan to Achieve the* Millennium Development Goals (New York: United Nations, 2005).

3. See Ethan B. Kapstein, "Reviving Aid," *World Policy Journal* 16 (Fall 1999): 35–44; for a good historical introduction to US foreign aid policy, see Carol Lancaster, "Foreign Aid: Diplomacy, Development, Domestic Politics" (manuscript, Georgetown University, 2005).

4. The best introduction to these issues remains World Bank, *Assessing Aid* (New York: Oxford University Press, 1998).

5. David Lumsdaine, *Moral Vision in International Politics: The Foreign Aid Regime, 1949–1989* (Princeton, NJ: Princeton University Press, 1993), p. 3.

6. Gunnar Myrdal, *The Equality Issue in World Development* (Oslo: Nobel Foundation, 17 March 1975), p. 8.

7. For more detail, see the Web site of the millennium challenge accounts at www.mca.gov.

8. Paul Collier and David Dollar, "Aid Allocation and Poverty Reduction" (World Bank Policy Research Working Paper no. 2041, January 1999), p. 11.

9. Jonathan Beynon, "Policy Implications for Aid Allocations of Recent Research on Aid Effectiveness and Selectivity" (paper presented at the Joint Development Center/DAC Ex-

perts Seminar on Aid Effectiveness, Selectivity and Poor Performers, OECD, Paris, 17 January 2001), p. 10.

10. Collier and Dollar, "Aid Allocation," p. 16.

11. Henrik Hansen and Finn Tarp, "Aid Effectiveness Disputed," *Journal of International Development* 12 (2000): 390.

12. Rawls, *Law of Peoples*, p. 106.

13. Ibid., p. 107.

14. Ibid., p. 108.

15. Ibid., p. 110.

16. Ibid., p. 113.

17. For a related argument, see Charles Lipson, *Reliable Partners: How Democracies Have Made a Separate Peace* (Princeton, NJ: Princeton University Press, 2003).

18. David Miller, "Justice and Global Inequality," in *Inequality, Globalization and World Politics*, ed. Andrew Hurrell and Ngaire Woods (Oxford: Oxford University Press, 1999), p. 203.

19. Humberto G. Llavador and John E. Roemer, "An Equal-Opportunity Approach to the Allocation of International Aid," *Journal of Development Economics* 64 (2001): 147–171.

20. Ibid., p. 148.

21. Organization for Economic Cooperation and Development (OECD), *Strengthening Trade Capacity for Development* (Paris: OECD, 2001), p. 20.

22. Richard Blackhurst, Bill Lyakurwa, and Ademola Oyejide, "Improving African Participation in the WTO" (paper commissioned by the World Bank for a conference at the WTO, 20–21 September 1999), p. 11.

23. Ibid., p. 13.

24. Dani Rodrik, *Making Openness Work* (Washington, DC: Overseas Development Council, 1999), p. 75.

25. Dani Rodrik, *Has Globalization Gone Too Far?* (Washington, DC: Institute for International Economics, 1997).

26. See Ethan B. Kapstein and Branko Milanovic, eds., *When Markets Fail: Social Policy and Economic Reform* (New York: Russell Sage Foundation, 2002).

CHAPTER FOUR
JUSTICE IN MIGRATION AND LABOR

Epigraph is from "Opening the Door," *The Economist*, 2 November 2002, p. 11.

1. I thank David Vogel for emphasizing this point.

2. For a good introduction, see Warren Schwartz, ed., *Justice in Immigration* (New York: Cambridge University Press, 2001).

3. For an excellent review of these issues, see Martin Ruhs and Ha-Joon Chang, "The Ethics of Labor Immigration Policy," *International Organization* 58 (Winter 2004): 69–102.

4. John Roemer, "The Non-Parochial Welfare Economics of Immigration" (manuscript, Yale University, 20 April 2001), p. 3.

5. See Ruhs and Chang, "Ethics of Labor Immigration Policy."

6. Myron Weiner, "Ethics, National Sovereignty and the Control of Immigration," *International Migration Review* 30, no. 1 (Spring 1996): 171.

7. Roemer, "Non-Parochial Welfare Economics of Immigration," p. 3.

8. See ibid.; Douglas Nelson and Yongsheng Xu, "Normative Migration Theory: A Social Choice Theoretic Approach" (manuscript, Tulane University, October 2001); and Andrés Solimano, "International Migration and the Global Economic Order" (World Bank Policy Research Working Paper 2720, November 2001).

9. John Rawls, *The Law of Peoples* (Cambridge, MA: Harvard University Press, 1999), pp. 8–9.

10. R. Albert Berry and Ronald Soligo, "Some Welfare Aspects of International Migration," *Journal of Political Economy* 77, no. 5 (September 1969): 778.

11. Solimano, "International Migration and the Global Economic Order," table 1.

12. Ibid., p. 16.

13. Ethan B. Kapstein, "Vicious or Virtuous Circles? Foreign Direct Investment and Human Capital Formation" (OECD Technical Papers, December 2001).

14. See United Nations, *World Economic and Social Survey: 1994* (New York: United Nations, 1994); this issue is devoted to the topic "international migration."

15. "Opening the Door," p. 11.

16. "The Would Be Europeans," *The Economist*, 4 August 1990, p. 15, cited in Weiner, "Ethics, National Sovereignty and the Control of Immigration," p. 182.

17. Weiner, "Ethics, National Sovereignty and the Control of Immigration," p. 173.

18. Michael Walzer, *Spheres of Justice* (New York: Basic Books, 1983).

19. I thank an anonymous reviewer for highlighting this point.

20. Solimano, "International Migration," p. 17.

21. Kevin H. O'Rourke and Jeffrey G. Williamson, *Globalization and History* (Cambridge, MA: MIT Press, 1999), p. 166.

22. Dani Rodrik, "Feasible Globalizations" (manuscript, Kennedy School of Government, Harvard University, 2002).

23. Indeed, Rodrik has a level of analysis problem in this piece, never making clear whether his main concern is a cosmopolitan or a liberal internationalist one.

24. For an exception, see Roemer, "Non-Parochial Welfare Economics of Immigration."

25. Ibid.

26. International Organization for Migration, "Making Migration a Win-Win Scenario" (paper presented at the World Economic Forum, Davos, Switzerland, 21 January 2004).

27. For a detailed description of some alternatives, see Mihir A. Desai, Devesh Kapur, and John McHale, "Sharing the Spoils: Taxing International Human Capital Flows" (Weatherhead Center for International Affairs Working Paper 02–06, Harvard University, September 2002).

28. Edmund Phelps, *Rewarding Work* (Cambridge, MA: Harvard University Press, 1997).

29. John Maynard Keynes, *The General Theory of Employment, Interest and Money* (1935; reprinted, New York: Harcourt Brace, 1964), p. 378.

30. Ibid., p. 383.

31. Dani Rodrik, "Labor Standards in International Trade: Do They Matter and What Do We Do about Them?" in *Emerging Agenda for Global Trade: High Stakes for Developing Countries*, ed. Robert Z. Lawrence, Dani Rodrik, and John Whalley (Washington, DC: Overseas Development Corporation, 1996), p. 42.

32. Cited in Ethan B. Kapstein, *Sharing the Wealth: Workers and the World Economy* (New York: Norton, 1999), p. 59.

33. For excellent surveys, see Nirvikar Singh, "The Impact of International Labor Standards: A Survey of Economic Theory" (manuscript, Department of Economics, University of California, Santa Cruz, October 2001), and Keith E. Maskus, "Should Core Labor Standards Be Imposed through International Trade Policy?" (paper prepared under contract to the World Bank, International Trade Division, August 1997).

34. See Singh, "Impact of International Labor Standards."

35. For important exceptions, see Rodrik, "Labor Standards in International Trade," and Richard Freeman, "International Labor Standards and World Trade: Friends or Foes?" in *Chal-*

lenge of the International Trading System, ed. Jeffrey Schott (Washington, DC: Institute for International Economics, 1996).

36. Ethan B. Kapstein, "The Corporate Ethics Crusade," *Foreign Affairs*, September/October 2001, p. 110.

37. See Eric Edmonds, "Does Child Labor Decline with Improving Economic Status?" (NBER Working Paper 10134, December 2003).

38. See Sandra Polaski, "Cambodia Blazes a New Path to Economic Growth and Job Creation" (Carnegie Papers 51, October 2004).

39. This point is also made by Stephen Golub, "International Labor Standards and International Trade" (IMF Working Paper WP/97/37, April 1997), p. 24.

40. My thinking along these lines has been influenced by Stephen Herzenberg, "In from the Margins: Morality, Economics, and International Labor Rights," in *Labor Rights, Human Rights, and International Trade*, ed. Lance Compa and Stephen Diamond (Philadelphia, PA: University of Pennsylvania Press, 1996), pp. 99–117.

CHAPTER FIVE
HARNESSING INVESTMENT

The epigraph is from Debora Spar and David Yoffie, "Multinational Enterprises and the Prospects for Justice," *Journal of International Affairs* 52, no. 2 (Spring 1999): 579.

1. Thomas Franck, *Fairness in International Law and Institutions* (New York: Oxford University Press, 1995), p. 438.

2. For a good review of the literature see Constantine V. Vaitsos, *Intercountry Income Distribution and Transnational Enterprises* (Oxford: Clarendon Press, 1974).

3. The best introduction to the topic remains Raymond Vernon, *Sovereignty at Bay* (New York: Basic Books, 1971).

4. Franck, *Fairness in International Law*, p. 441.

5. Vaitsos, *Intercountry Income Distribution*.

6. Franck, *Fairness in International Law*, p. 444.

7. For an analysis of these ethical issues that remains timely despite its date of publication, see Thomas Donaldson, "Moral Minimums for Multinationals," *Ethics and International Affairs* 3 (1989): 163–182; for a skeptical view of corporate social responsibility, see Ethan B. Kapstein, "The Corporate Ethics Crusade," *Foreign Affairs*, August/September 2001, pp. 105–119.

8. Alfred Chandler, *The Visible Hand* (Cambridge, MA: Harvard University Press, 1974).

9. Peter Evans, *Dependent Development: The Alliance of Multinational, State, and Local Capital in Brazil* (Princeton, NJ: Princeton University Press, 1979).

10. Charles P. Kindleberger, *American Business Abroad* (New Haven, CT: Yale University Press, 1969), p. 149.

11. Ibid.

12. Vaitsos, *Intercountry Income Distribution*.

13. E. T. Penrose, "Profit Sharing between Producing Companies and Oil Countries in the Middle East," *Economic Journal* 69 (June 1959): 238–254, cited in Kindleberger, *American Business Abroad*, p. 149.

14. Kindleberger, *American Business Abroad*, p. 154.

15. Ibid., p. 157.

16. Ibid., p. 177.

17. Vernon, *Sovereignty at Bay*.

18. James Markusen, "Multilateral Rules on Foreign Direct Investment: The Developing Countries' Stake" (study prepared for the World Bank, 7 October 1998), p. 48.

19. A point emphasized by Robert Axelrod in *The Evolution of Cooperation* (New York: Basic Books, 1984).

20. Kenneth Abbott and Duncan Snidal, "International Standards and International Governance" (Harris School

Working Papers 00.18, University of Chicago, 1 February 2000), p. 9.

21. Kindleberger, *American Business Abroad*, p. 158.

22. Markusen, "Multilateral Rules on Foreign Direct Investment," p. 45.

23. Ibid., p. 46.

24. Edward M. Graham, *Fighting the Wrong Enemy: Antiglobal Activists and Multinational Enterprises* (Washington, DC: Institute for International Economics, 2000), p. 171.

25. Ethan B. Kapstein, *Governing the Global Economy: International Finance and the State* (Cambridge, MA: Harvard University Press, 1994).

26. Adapted from Ajit Singh, *Foreign Direct Investment and International Agreements: A South Perspective* (Geneva: South Centre, October 2001), p. 5.

27. Graham, *Fighting the Wrong Enemy*, p. 67.

28. Melvin L. Burstein and Arthur J. Rolnick, "Congress Should End the Economic War among the States," *The Region* (Minneapolis: Federal Reserve of Minneapolis, March 1995), available at http://minneapolisfed.org/pubs/ar/ar1994.cfm. It should be emphasized that these authors and others believe that Congress *could* bring an end to this "war" if it wished to do so, so the problem is not found in the *legal* structure of the United States.

29. Raymond Vernon, *In the Hurricane's Eye: The Troubled Prospects of Multinational Enterprises* (Cambridge, MA: Harvard University Press, 1998), p. 210.

30. See the discussion in Graham, *Fighting the Wrong Enemy*, pp. 180–182.

31. Oxfam, "Update on the Proposed Multilateral Agreement on Investment," (April 1998), at www.oxfam.org.uk/policy/papers/maiapr98/maiapr98.html.

32. Thomas Gresik, "The Taxing Task of Taxing Multinationals," *Journal of Economic Literature* 39 (September 2001): 800–838.

33. John Gerard Ruggie, "Taking Embedded Liberalism Global: The Corporate Connection," in *Global Economic Governance*, ed. David Held and Mathias Koenig-Archibugi (Oxford: Polity Press, forthcoming).

34. Spar and Yoffie, "Multinational Enterprises and the Prospects for Justice," pp. 575–578.

35. Ibid., p. 578.

36. Michael Klein, Carl Aaron, and Bita Hadjimichael, "Foreign Direct Investment and Poverty Reduction" (prepared for the World Bank, n.d.).

37. Ruggie, "Taking Embedded Liberalism Global."

38. Georg Kell and David Levin, "The Evolution of the Global Compact Network: An Historical Experiment in Learning and Action" (report, United Nations Global Compact office, June 2001), p. 1.

39. Ibid., p. 4.

40. Ruggie, "Taking Embedded Liberalism Global."

41. Ibid.

42. Ibid.

43. Kell and Levin, "Evolution of the Global Compact," p. 5.

44. Franck, *Fairness in International Law*, p. 472.

CHAPTER SIX
TOWARD A LEVEL PLAYING FIELD

The epigraph is from Gunnar Myrdal, *The Equality Issue in World Development* (Oslo: Nobel Foundation, 1975), p. 11.

1. United Nations Millennium Project, *Investing in Development: A Practical Plan to Achieve the Millennium Development Goals* (New York: United Nations, 2005).

2. World Bank, *Poverty Reduction and the World Bank* (Washington, D.C.: World Bank, 1996).

3. Details of these negotiations can be found on the WTO Web site at www.wto.org.

4. Available at www.imf.org/external/np/sec/pn/2002/pn0230.htm.

5. Available at www.imf.org/external/np/sec/pn/2002/pn0230.htm.

6. See Martha Finnemore, *National Interests in International Society* (Ithaca, NY: Cornell University Press, 1996), and Margaret Keck and Kathryn Sikkink, *Activists beyond Borders* (Ithaca, NY: Cornell University Press 1999).

7. Alexander Wendt, "Anarchy Is What States Make of It: The Social Construction of Power Politics," *International Organization* 46, no. 3 (Spring 1992): 391–426.

8. See Finnemore, *National Interests in International Society.*

9. Available at www.imf.org/external/np/sec/pn/2002/pn0230.htm.

10. Available at www.imf.org/external/np/sec/pn/2002/pn0230.htm.

11. Samuel P. Huntington, *Political Order in Changing Societies* (New Haven, CT: Yale University Press, 1968), p. 344.

12. Ibid.

13. Kenneth Boulding, "Defense and Opulence: The Ethics of International Economics," *American Economic Review* 41, no. 2 (May 1951): 216.

BIBLIOGRAPHY

Abbott, Kenneth, and Duncan Snidal. "International Standards and International Governance." Harris School Working Papers 00.18, University of Chicago, 1 February 2000.

Acemoglu, Daron, Simon Johnson, and James Robinson. "Reversal of Fortune: Geography and Institutions in the Making of the Modern World Income Distribution." Manuscript, 9 August 2001.

Acemoglu, Daron, and James Robinson. "Political Origins of Democracy and Dictatorship." Manuscript, 2003.

Acemoglu, Daron, and Jaume Ventura. "The World Income Distribution." NBER Working Paper 8083, 2001.

Albin, Cecilia. *Justice and Fairness in International Negotiation*. New York: Cambridge University Press, 2001.

Arndt, H. W. *Essays in International Economics: 1944–1994*. Aldershot, UK: Avebury, 1995.

Arneson, Richard. "Economic Analysis Meets Distributive Justice." *Social Theory and Practice* 26, no. 2 (Summer 2000): 1–15.

Axelrod, Robert. *The Evolution of Cooperation*. New York. Basic Books, 1984.

Baldwin, Richard E., Henrik Braconier, and Rikard Forslid. "Multinationals, Endogenous Growth and Technological Spillovers: Theory and Evidence." Manuscript, August 1999.

Bannister, Geoffrey J., and Kamau Thugge. "International Trade and Poverty Alleviation." IMF Working Paper WP/01/54, May 2001.

Barkan, Elazar. *The Guilt of Nations*. Baltimore: Johns Hopkins University Press, 2001.

Barnett, Laura. *Global Governance and the Evolution of the International Refugee Regime*. Geneva: United Nations High Commission for Refugees, 2002.

Barry, Christian. "Global Justice: Aims, Arrangements, and Responsibilities." In *Can Institutions Have Duties?* ed. Toni Erskine. London: Palgrave, 2003.

Baumol, William. *Superfairness.* Cambridge, MA: MIT Press, 1988.

Beitz, Charles. "International Liberalism and Distributive Justice: A Survey of Recent Thought." *World Politics* 51 (January 1999): 269–296.

————. *Political Theory and International Relations.* Princeton, NJ: Princeton University Press, 1979.

Beitz, Charles. ed. *International Ethics.* Princeton, NJ: Princeton University Press, 1985.

Ben-David, Dan. *Trade, Growth, and Disparity among Nations.* Geneva: World Trade Organization, 1999.

Berry, R. Albert, and Ronald Soligo. "Some Welfare Aspects of International Migration." *Journal of Political Economy* 77, no. 5 (September 1969): 778–794.

Beynon, Jonathan. "Policy Implications for Aid Allocations of Recent Research on Aid Effectiveness and Selectivity." Paper presented at the Joint Development Center/DAC Experts Seminar on Aid Effectiveness, Selectivity and Poor Performers, OECD, Paris, 17 January 2001.

Bhagwati, Jagdish. "Free Trade: Why the AFL-CIO, the Sierra Club, and Congressman Gephardt Should Like It." Remarks presented on receiving the Seidman Award in Political Economy, 18 September 1998.

Bhagwati, Jagdish, and T. N. Srinivasan. "Trade and Poverty in the Poor Countries." Manuscript, December 2001.

Blackhurst, Richard, Bill Lyakurwa, and Ademola Oyejide. "Improving African Participation in the WTO." Paper commissioned by the World Bank for a conference at the World Trade Organization, 20–21 September 1999.

Blumenthal, Monica D., et al. *More about Justifying Violence: Methodological Studies of Attitudes and Behavior.* Ann Arbor, MI: Institute for Social Research, University of Michigan, 1975.

Bolton, Gary, et al. "Testing Theories of Other-Regarding Behavior: A Sequence of Four Laboratory Studies." Manuscript, n.d.

Boulding, Kenneth. "Defense and Opulence: The Ethics of International Economics." *American Economic Review* 41, no. 2 (May 1951): 210–220.

Brecher, Richard, and Ehsan Choudhri. "Pareto Gains from Trade Reconsidered: Compensating for Jobs Lost." *Journal of International Economics* 36, no. 3 (1994): 223–238.

Brettell, Caroline, and James F. Hollifield, eds. *Migration Theory: Talking across Disciplines*. New York: Routledge, 2000.

Brown, Chris. "Moral Agency and International Society." *Ethics and International Affairs* 15, no. 2 (2001): 87–98.

Bueno de Mesquita, Bruce, and David Lalman. *War and Reason*. New Haven, CT: Yale University Press, 1992.

Bull, Hedley. *The Anarchical Society*. New York: Columbia University Press, 1977.

Caney, Simon. "International Distributive Justice." *Political Studies* 49 (2001): 974–997.

Carr, E. H. *The Twenty Years' Crisis*. 1939; reprinted, New York: Harper and Row, 1962.

Caves, Richard. *Multinational Enterprise and Economic Analysis*. New York: Cambridge University Press, 1995.

Chan, Kenneth S. "The International Negotiation Game: Some Evidence from the Tokyo Round." *Review of Economics and Statistics* 67, no. 3 (Autumn 1985): 456–464.

Chandler, Alfred D. *The Visible Hand*. Cambridge, MA: Harvard University Press, 1974.

Clark, Don. "Are Poorer Developing Countries the Targets of U.S. Protectionist Actions?" *Economic Development and Cultural Change*, October 1998, pp. 193–207.

Cline, William. *Trade and Income Distribution*. Washington, DC: Institute for International Economics, 1997.

Collier, Paul, and David Dollar. "Aid Allocation and Poverty Reduction." World Bank Policy Research Working Paper no. 2041, January 1999. At www.worldbank.org/research/abcde/washington_11/pdfs/collier.pdf.

Cooke, Alistair, ed. *Mencken*. New York: Knopf, 1955.

Copeland, Dale. "Economic Interdependence and War: A Theory of Trade Expectations." *International Security* 20, no. 4 (Spring 1996): 5–41.

Desai, Mihir A., Devesh Kapur, and John McHale. "Sharing the Spoils: Taxing International Human Capital Flows." Weatherhead Center for International Affairs Working Paper 02–06, Harvard University, September 2002.

Diamond, Jared. *Guns, Germs, and Steel*. New York: Norton, 1998.

Dickins, Amanda. "Just Distributions: Economic Globalisation and International Distributive Justice." Paper presented at the annual meeting of the American Political Science Association, Boston, August 2002.

Dollar, David, and Aart Kraay. "Trade, Growth and Poverty." World Bank Policy Research Working Papers no. 2615, 1 June 2001.

Donaldson, Thomas. "Moral Minimums for Multinationals." *Ethics and International Affairs* 3 (1989): 163–182.

Doyle, Michael. *Ways of War and Peace*. New York: Norton, 1997.

Dworkin, Ronald. *Sovereign Virtue*. Princeton, NJ: Princeton University Press, 2000.

Easterly, William. *The Elusive Quest for Growth*. Cambridge, MA: MIT Press, 2001.

Eberstadt, Nicholas. "The Future of AIDS." *Foreign Affairs*, November/December 2002, pp. 22–45.

Edmonds, Eric. "Does Child Labor Decline with Improving Economic Status?" NBER Working Paper 10134, December 2003.

Evans, Peter. *Dependent Development: The Alliance of Multinational, State, and Local Capital in Brazil*. Princeton, NJ: Princeton University Press, 1979.

Fehr, Ernst, and Simon Gachter. "Fairness and Retaliation: The Economics of Reciprocity." *Journal of Economic Perspectives* 14, no. 3 (Summer 2000): 159–181.

Finger, J. Michael, Ulrich Reincke, and Adriana Castro. "Market Access Bargaining in the Uruguay Round: Rigid or Relaxed Reciprocity?" World Bank Working Paper no. 2258 (1999).

Finnemore, Martha. *National Interests in International Society.* Ithaca, NY: Cornell University Press, 1996.

Finnemore, Martha, and Kathryn Sikkink. "International Norm Dynamics and Political Change." *International Organization* 52, no. 4 (Autumn 1998): 887–917.

Franck, Thomas. *Fairness in International Law and Institutions.* New York: Oxford University Press, 1995.

Freeman, Richard. "International Labor Standards and World Trade: Friends or Foes?" In *Challenge of the International Trading System*, ed. Jeffrey Schott. Washington, DC: Institute for International Economics, 1996.

Friedman, Benjamin. "What Is Poverty?" *New York Review of Books*, 21 November 2002, p. 62.

Fukuyama, Francis. *The End of History and the Last Man.* New York: Basic Books, 1992.

Gauthier, David. *Morals by Agreement.* Oxford: Clarendon Press, 1986.

Gilpin, Robert. *U.S. Power and the Multinational Corporation.* New York: Basic Books, 1974.

Golub, Stephen. "International Labor Standards and International Trade." IMF Working Paper WP/97/37, April 1997.

Graham, Edward M. *Fighting the Wrong Enemy: Antiglobal Activists and Multinational Enterprises.* Washington, DC: Institute for International Economics, 2000.

Greif, Avner. "Contract Enforceability and Economic Institutions in Early Trade: The Maghribi Traders' Coalition." *American Economic Review* 83, no. 3 (1993): 525–548.

Gresik, Thomas. "The Taxing Task of Taxing Multinationals." *Journal of Economic Literature* 39 (September 2001): 800–838.

Gresser, Edward. "Toughest on the Poor." *Foreign Affairs*, November/December 2002, pp. 9–14.

Grimwade, Nigel. *International Trade Policy: A Contemporary Analysis.* New York: Routledge, 1996.

Grossman, Gene, and Elhanan Helpman. *Special Interest Politics.* Cambridge, MA: MIT Press, 2001.

Haberger, Arnold. "A Vision of the Growth Process." *American Economic Review* 88, no. 1 (March 1998): 1–32.

Hampshire, Stuart. *Justice Is Conflict.* Princeton, NJ: Princeton University Press, 2000.

Hansen, Henrik, and Finn Tarp. "Aid Effectiveness Disputed." *Journal of International Development* 12 (2000): 375–398.

Hardt, Michael, and Antonio Negri. *Empire.* Cambridge, MA: Harvard University Press, 2002.

Harris, Paul G., and Patricia Siplon. "International Obligation and Human Health: Evolving Policy Responses to HIV/AIDS." *Ethics and International Affairs* 15, no. 2 (2001): 29–52.

Harrison, Glenn W., Thomas F. Rutherford, and David G. Tarr. "Quantifying the Uruguay Round." In *The Uruguay Round and Developing Countries*, ed. Will Martin and L. Alan Winters. Washington, DC: World Bank, 1995.

Hausman, Daniel, and Michael McPherson. *Economic Analysis and Moral Philosophy.* New York: Cambridge University Press, 1996.

Herzenberg, Stephen. "In from the Margins: Morality, Economics, and International Labor Rights." In *Labor Rights, Human Rights, and International Trade*, ed. Lance Compa and Stephen Diamond. Philadelphia: University of Pennsylvania Press, 1996.

Hirschman, Albert O. *Journeys towards Progress.* New York: Twentieth Century Fund, 1963.

Hirshleifer, Jack. *The Dark Side of the Force.* New York: Cambridge University Press, 2001.

Hoffmann, Stanley. *Duties beyond Borders.* Syracuse, NY: Syracuse University Press, 1981.

Howe, Roger, and John Roemer. "Rawlsian Justice as the Core of a Game." *American Economic Review* 71 (December 1981): 880–895.

Hudec, Robert. *Developing Countries in the GATT Legal System*. London: Trade Policy Research Centre, 1987.

Huntington, Samuel P. *Political Order in Changing Societies*. New Haven, CT: Yale University Press, 1968.

Hurrell, Andrew. "Power, Institutions, and the Production of Inequality." In *Power in Global Governance*, ed. Michael Barnett and Raymond Duvall. New York: Cambridge University Press, 2005.

Hurrell, Andrew, and Ngaire Woods. *Inequality, Globalization and World Politics*. Oxford: Oxford University Press, 1999.

Ikenberry, G. John. *After Victory*. Princeton, NJ: Princeton University Press, 2002.

Ikenberry, G. John, and Charles A. Kupchan. "Socialization and Hegemonic Power." *International Organization* 44, no. 3 (Summer 1990): 283–315.

International Monetary Fund. *World Economic Outlook*, May 2002.

International Monetary Fund and World Bank. "Market Access for Developing Countries' Exports." Electronic manuscript, 27 April 2001. Posted at www.imf.org/external/np/madc/eng/042701.htm.

International Organization for Migration. "Making Migration a Win-Win Scenario." Paper presented at the World Economic Forum, Davos, Switzerland, 21 January 2004.

Irwin, Douglas. *Against the Tide: An Intellectual History of Free Trade*. Princeton, NJ: Princeton University Press, 1996.

Jones, Charles I. *Introduction to Economic Growth*. New York. Norton, 1998.

Joppke, Christian. "Why Liberal States Accept Unwanted Immigration." *World Politics* 50, no. 2 (January 1998): 266–293.

Kanbur, Ravi. "Development Economics and the Compensation Principle." Manuscript, Cornell University, 2002.

Kanbur, Ravi, and Lynn Squire. "The Evolution of Thinking about Poverty." Manuscript, Cornell University, 1999.

Kapstein, Ethan B. "The Corporate Ethics Crusade." *Foreign Affairs*, September/October 2001, pp. 105–119.

Kapstein, Ethan B. *Governing the Global Economy: International Finance and the State*. Cambridge, MA: Harvard University Press, 1994.

———. "Reviving Aid." *World Policy Journal* 16 (Fall 1999): 35–44.

———. *Sharing the Wealth: Workers and the World Economy*. New York: Norton, 1999.

———. "Vicious or Virtuous Circles? Foreign Direct Investment and Human Capital Formation." OECD Technical Papers, December 2001.

Kapstein, Ethan, and Branko Milanovic. *Income and Influence*. Kalamazoo, MI: Upjohn Institute, 2003.

———, eds. *When Markets Fail: Social Policy and Economic Reform*. New York: Russell Sage Foundation, 2002.

Katzenstein, Peter J., ed. *Between Power and Plenty*. Madison: University of Wisconsin Press, 1978.

Keck, Margaret, and Kathryn Sikkink. *Activists beyond Borders*. Ithaca, NY: Cornell University Press, 1999.

Keohane, Robert. *After Hegemony: Cooperation and Discord in the World Political Economy*. Princeton, NJ: Princeton University Press, 1984.

———. "Reciprocity in International Relations." *International Organization* 40, no. 1 (Winter 1986): 1–27.

Keynes, John Maynard. *The General Theory of Employment, Interest and Money*. 1935; reprinted, New York: Harcourt Brace, 1964.

Kindleberger, Charles P. *American Business Abroad*. New Haven, CT: Yale University Press, 1969.

Knight, Jack. *Institutions and Social Conflict*. New York: Cambridge University Press, 1992.

Koremenos, Barbara, Charles Lipson, and Duncan Snidal. "The Rational Design of International Institutions." *International Organization* 55, no. 1 (Autumn 2001): 1051–1082.

Krasner, Stephen D. *Structural Conflict: The Third World against Global Liberalization*. Berkeley and Los Angeles: University of California Press, 1985.

————, ed. *International Regimes*. Ithaca, NY: Cornell University Press, 1983.

Krueger, Anne. *Trade Policies and Developing Nations*. Washington, DC: Brookings Institution, 1995.

Krugman, Paul. "A Model of Innovation, Technology Transfer, and the World Distribution of Income." *Journal of Political Economy* 87 (April 1979): 253–266.

Krugman, Paul, and Maurice Obstfeld. *International Economics*. Reading, MA: Addison-Wesley, 2000.

Lancaster, Carol. "Foreign Aid: Diplomacy, Development, Domestic Politics." Manuscript, Georgetown University, 2005.

Landa, Dimitri, and Ethan Kapstein. "Inequality, Growth and Democracy." *World Politics* 53 (January 2001): 264–296.

Lawrence, Robert Z., Dani Rodrik, and John Whalley, eds. *Emerging Agenda for Global Trade: High Stakes for Developing Countries*. Washington, DC: Overseas Development Council, 1996.

Levine, Ruth. *Millions Saved: Proven Successes in Global Health*. Washington, DC: Center for Global Development, 2004.

Lewis, David. *Convention: A Philosophical Study*. Cambridge, MA: Harvard University Press, 1969.

Lewis, John P. "Oil, Other Scarcities, and the Poor Countries." *World Politics* 27 (1974): 63–86.

Lichbach, Mark Irving, and Alan S. Zuckerman, eds. *Comparative Politics*. New York: Cambridge University Press, 1997.

Lipson, Charles. *Reliable Partners: How Democracies Have Made a Separate Peace*. Princeton, NJ: Princeton University Press, 2003.

Llavador, Humberto G., and John E. Roemer. "An Equal-Opportunity Approach to the Allocation of International Aid." *Journal of Development Economics* 64 (2001): 147–171.

Lumsdaine, David. *Moral Vision in International Politics: The Foreign Aid Regime, 1949–1989*. Princeton, NJ: Princeton University Press, 1993.

Mansfield, Edward. *Power, Trade, and War.* Princeton, NJ: Princeton University Press, 1994.

Markusen, James. "Multilateral Rules on Foreign Direct Investment: The Developing Countries' Stake." Study prepared for the World Bank, 7 October 1998.

Martin, Will, and L. Alan Winters, eds. *The Uruguay Round and Developing Countries.* Washington, DC: World Bank, 1995.

Maskus, Keith E. "Should Core Labor Standards Be Imposed through International Trade Policy?" Paper prepared under contract to the World Bank, International Trade Division, August 1997.

McCulloch, Niel, L. Alan Winters, and Xavier Cirera. *Trade Liberalization and Poverty: A Handbook.* London: Centre for Economic Policy Research, 2001.

Meade, James. *The Theory of International Economic Policy, Trade and Welfare.* New York: Oxford University Press, 1955.

Meier, Gerald M. *International Trade and Development.* New York: Harper and Row, 1963.

Mersterton-Gibbons, Michael, and Eldridge S. Adams. "The Economics of Animal Cooperation." *Science,* 13 December 2002, pp. 2146–2147.

Milanovic, Branko. "True World Income Distribution, 1988 and 1993: First Calculation Based on Household Surveys Alone." Manuscript, World Bank, Development Research Group, 2000.

———. "Worlds Apart." Manuscript, World Bank, Development Research Group, 2002.

Mill, John Stuart. *Principles of Political Economy.* 1848; reprinted, New York: Penguin, 1979.

Miller, David. "Justice and Global Inequality." In *Inequality, Globalization and World Politics,* ed. Andrew Hurrell and Ngaire Woods. Oxford. Oxford University Press, 1999.

Myrdal, Gunnar. *The Equality Issue in World Development.* Oslo: Nobel Foundation, 1975.

Nadelmann, Ethan. "Global Prohibition Regimes: The Evolution of Norms in International Society." *International Organization* 44, no. 4 (Autumn 1990): 479–526.

Nelson, Douglas, and Yongsheng Xu. "Normative Migration Theory: A Social Choice Theoretic Approach." Manuscript, Tulane University, October 2001.

Nowak, Martin A., Karen Page, and Karl Sigmund. "Fairness versus Reason in the Ultimatum Game." *Science*, 8 September 2000, pp. 1773–1775.

Nozick, Robert. *Anarchy, State and Utopia.* New York: Basic Books, 1974.

O'Connor, Alice. *Poverty Knowledge: Social Science, Social Policy, and the Poor in Twentieth-Century U.S. History.* Princeton, NJ: Princeton University Press, 2001.

"Opening the Door." *The Economist*, 2 November 2002, p. 11.

Organization for Economic Cooperation and Development (OECD). *Strengthening Trade Capacity for Development.* Paris: OECD, 2001.

———. *Trade, Employment and Labor Standards.* Paris: OECD, 1996.

O'Rourke, Kevin H., and Jeffrey G. Williamson. *Globalization and History.* Cambridge, MA: MIT Press, 1999.

Oxfam. *Rigged Rules and Double Standards: Trade, Globalization and the Fight against Poverty.* Oxford: Oxfam, 2002.

Packenham, Robert. *Liberal America and the Third World.* Princeton, NJ: Princeton University Press, 1973.

Parfit, Derek. "Equality and Priority." *Ratio* 10, no. 3 (December 1997): 202–221.

Parisi, Francesco, and Nita Ghei. "The Role of Reciprocity in International Law." Manuscript, George Mason University School of Law, n.d.

Penrose, E. T. "Profit Sharing between Producing Companies and Oil Countries in the Middle East." *Economic Journal* 69 (June 1959): 238–254.

Phelps, E. S. *Economic Justice.* Baltimore: Penguin, 1973.

Phelps, E. S. *Rewarding Work*. Cambridge, MA: Harvard University Press, 1997.

Pogge, Thomas. "Cosmopolitanism and Sovereignty." *Ethics* 103 (October 1992): 48–75.

————. "An Egalitarian Law of Peoples." *Philosophy & Public Affairs* 23, no. 3 (Summer 1994): 195–224.

————. "Moral Universalism and Global Economic Justice." *Politics, Philosophy and Economics* 1 (February 2002): 29–58.

————, ed. *Global Justice*. Oxford: Blackwell, 2001.

Polaski, Sandra. "Cambodia Blazes a New Path to Economic Growth and Job Creation." Carnegie Papers 51, October 2004.

Powell, Robert. "Bargaining Theory and International Conflict." Manuscript, University of California, Berkeley, 2004.

Puchala, Donald J., and Raymond F. Hopkins. "International Regimes: Lessons from Inductive Analysis." In *International Regimes*, ed. Stephen D. Krasner. Ithaca, NY: Cornell University Press, 1983.

Putnam, Robert D. "Diplomacy and Domestic Politics: The Logic of Two-Level Games." *International Organization* 42, no. 3 (Summer 1988): 427–460.

Rawls, John. *The Law of Peoples*. Cambridge, MA: Harvard University Press, 1999.

————. *A Theory of Justice*. Cambridge, MA: Harvard University Press, 1971.

Reddy, Sanjay, and Thomas Pogge. "How *Not* to Count the Poor." Electronic manuscript, 2002. Posted at www.socialanalysis.org.

Richardson, J. David. *Understanding International Trade*. Boston: Little, Brown, 1980.

Risse, Mathias. "Do We Live in an Unjust World?" Faculty Research Working Papers, RWP03–049, Kennedy School of Government, Harvard University, December 2003.

Rodrik, Dani. "Feasible Globalizations." NBER Working Paper W9129, August 2002.

————. *Has Globalization Gone Too Far?* Washington, DC: Institute for International Economics, 1997.

————. "Labor Standards in International Trade: Do They Matter and What Do We Do about Them?" In *Emerging Agenda for Global Trade: High Stakes for Developing Countries*, ed. Robert Z. Lawrence, Dani Rodrik, and John Whalley. Washington, DC: Overseas Development Corporation, 1996.

————. *Making Openness Work.* Washington, DC: Overseas Development Council, 1999.

Roemer, John E. *Equality of Opportunity.* Cambridge, MA: Harvard University Press, 1998.

————. "The Non-Parochial Welfare Economics of Immigration." Manuscript, Yale University, 20 April 2001.

Ruggie, John. "International Regimes, Transactions, and Change: Embedded Liberalism in the Postwar Economic Order." In *International Regimes*, ed. Stephen D. Krasner. Ithaca, NY: Cornell University Press, 1983.

————. "Taking Embedded Liberalism Global: The Corporate Connection." In *Global Economic Governance*, ed. David Held and Mathias Koenig-Archibugi (Oxford: Polity Press, forthcoming).

————. "What Makes the World Hang Together? Neo-Utilitarianism and the Social Constructivist Challenge." *International Organization* 52, no. 4 (Autumn 1998): 855–885.

Ruhs, Martin, and Ha-Joon Chang. "The Ethics of Labor Immigration Policy." *International Organization* 58 (Winter 2004): 69–102.

Sachs, Jeffrey, and Andrew Warner. "Economic Reform and the Process of Global Integration." *Brookings Papers on Economic Activity* 1 (1995): 1–118.

Sagan, Scott. "Realist Perspectives on Ethical Norms." Manuscript, Stanford University, 2004.

Samuelson, Paul. "International Factor Price Equalization Once Again." *Economic Journal* 59 (June 1949): 181–197.

Samuelson, Paul. "International Trade and the Equalization of Factor Prices." *Economic Journal* 58 (June 1948): 163–183.

Schelling, Thomas. *Choice and Consequences.* Cambridge, MA: Harvard University Press, 1984.

———. *The Strategy of Conflict.* Cambridge, MA: Harvard University Press, 1960.

Schott, Jeffrey. *Challenge of the International Trading System.* Washington, DC: Institute for International Economics, 1996.

Schwartz, Warren, ed. *Justice in Immigration.* New York: Cambridge University Press, 2001.

Sen, Amartya. *Inequality Reexamined.* Cambridge, MA: Harvard University Press, 1992.

———. *Poverty and Famines: An Essay on Entitlement and Deprivation.* Oxford: Clarendon Press, 1981.

Shaw, Brent. "Loving the Poor." *New York Review of Books*, 21 November 2002, pp. 42–45.

Sherman, Edward. "Endogenous Protection and Trade Negotiations." Electronic manuscript, Maxwell School, Syracuse University, n.d. At www.maxwell.syr.edu/maxpages/faculty/sherman/papers.html.

Singer, Peter. "Famine, Affluence, and Morality." In *International Ethics*, ed. Charles Beitz. Princeton, NJ: Princeton University Press, 1985.

———. *One World: The Ethics of Globalization.* New Haven, CT: Yale University Press, 2002.

Singh, Ajit. *Foreign Direct Investment and International Agreements: A South Perspective.* Geneva: South Centre, 2001.

Singh, Nirvikar. "The Impact of International Labor Standards: A Survey of Economic Theory." Manuscript, Department of Economics, University of California, Santa Cruz, October 2001.

Solimano, Andrés. "International Migration and the Global Economic Order." World Bank Policy Research Working Paper 2720, November 2001.

Spar, Debora, and David Yoffie. "Multinational Enterprises and the Prospects for Justice." *Journal of International Affairs* 52, no. 2 (Spring 1999): 557–581.

Srinivasan, T. N. *Developing Countries and the Multilateral Trading System.* Boulder, CO: Westview Press, 1998.

———. "Trade and Development: Developing Countries in the World Trading System: 1947–1999." Manuscript, Yale University, May 1999.

Stiglitz, Joseph. "A Fair Deal for the World." *New York Review of Books,* 23 May 2002, pp. 15–20.

Thomas, John R. "HIV/AIDS Drugs, Patents, and the TRIPS Agreement: Issues and Options." In *CRS Report for Congress.* Washington, DC: Library of Congress, 27 July 2001.

Trollope, Anthony. *The Way We Live Now.* 1875; reprinted, New York: Modern Library, 2001.

United Nations. *World Economic and Social Survey: 1994.* New York: United Nations, 1994.

United Nations. *World Economic and Social Survey: 1994.* New York: United Nations, 1994.

United Nations Development Program. *Globalization with a Human Face.* New York: Oxford University Press, 1999.

United Nations Millennium Project. *Investing in Development: A Practical Plan to Achieve the Millennium Development Goals.* New York: United Nations, 2005.

Vaitsos, Constantine V. *Intercountry Income Distribution and Transnational Enterprises.* Oxford: Clarendon Press, 1974.

Varian, Hal. "Distributive Justice, Welfare Economics and the Theory of Fairness." *Philosophy and Public Affairs* 4 (Spring 1975): 223–247.

Vernon, Raymond. *In the Hurricane's Eye: The Troubled Prospects of Multinational Enterprises.* Cambridge, MA: Harvard University Press, 1998.

———. *Sovereignty at Bay.* New York: Basic Books, 1971.

Walzer, Michael. *Spheres of Justice.* New York: Basic Books, 1983.

Weiner, Myron. "Ethics, National Sovereignty and the Control of Immigration." *International Migration Review* 30, no. 1 (Spring 1996): 171–197.

Wendt, Alexander. "Anarchy Is What States Make of It: The Social Construction of Power Politics." *International Organization* 46, no. 3 (Spring 1992): 391–426.

Wilson, E. O. "The Biological Basis of Morality." *Atlantic*, April 1998, pp. 53–78.

Wood, Adrian. *North-South Trade, Employment and Inequality.* New York. Oxford University Press, 1994.

World Bank. *Assessing Aid.* New York: Oxford University Press, 1998.

———. *Poverty Reduction and the World Bank.* Washington, DC: World Bank, 1996.

Youssef, Hesham. *Special and Differential Treatment for Developing Countries in the WTO.* Geneva: South Centre, n.d.

INDEX

activism, 1, 12; AIDS and, 77; child labor and, 142–43; corporate social responsibility and, 164–68; Global Reporting Initiative and, 165–66; labor standards and, 140; multinational enterprises (MNEs) and, 147–49; pharmaceutical products and, 48

agriculture, xi; GATT and, 67–69; balance-of-payments support and, 109–11; genetically-modified crops and, 116; liberal internationalism and, 59–60, 64–71 (*see also* liberal internationalism); protectionism and, 1, 65. *See also* labor

AIDS: cosmopolitanism and, 74–75, 77–79; NGOs and, 72–73; pharmaceuticals and, 48, 71–79; policy proposals for, 75–79; South Africa and, 71–75

Amnesty International, 147

anarchy, 30

Annan, Kofi, 169

Apparel Industry Partnership, 165

Asian tigers, 92

Axelrod, Robert, 30

balance-of-payments, 109–12

balance-of-power theory, 27–28

Bangladesh, 59, 94

bargaining theory, 202n69; changing terms and, 155; foreign direct investment (FDI) and, 151–57; game theory and, 156–57; host country advantages and, 153; Kindleberger and, 152–55; Multilateral Agreement on Investment (MAI) and, 157; mutual advantage and, 153; TAPLINE and, 154–55

beggar-thy-neighbor approach, 111

Beitz, Charles, 15, 19, 39, 53–54

Berry, Albert, 120

bilateral investment treaties (BITs), 159

Blackhurst, Richard, 106

Boulding, Kenneth, 46, 194–95

Brazil, 149, 159

Brecher, Richard, 82

Bretton Woods conference, 7, 66

Brown, Gordon, 12–13
Bueno de Mesquita, Bruce, 27
Bush, George W., 90

Canada, 127
Cancun trade summit, 84
Carr, E. H., 1, 34
Catholic Church, 177, 179
Chad, 26
Chan, Kenneth, 60–62
Chicago school of economics, 166–67
child labor, 24, 142–43
Chile, 94
China, 20–21, 29, 149, 164, 179
Chirac, Jacques, 13
Choudhri, Ehsan, 82
civil liberties, 21
Cline, William, 8
Clinton administration, 21
Collier, Paul, 91–96
Communist societies, 92, 96, 135
communitarianism, 3, 6, 74–76; domestic policies and, 8; education and, 9–10; escape clauses and, 7–8; international policies and, 8–10; migration and, 118, 125; openness effects and, 9–10; poverty and, 7, 176–84; rules-based regimes and, 9
consequentialism, 16, 137
constructivism, 178–79

convergence: equality of opportunity and, 40, 101–7; migration and, 128–31
cooperation theories: game theory and, 30–37 (see also game theory); international relations theory and, 30–44; reciprocity and, 30–44; tit-for-tat strategy and, 30; World Trade Organization and, 30–31
core labor standards (CLS), 138–39
corporate responsibility, 164–68
cosmopolitanism, 3; AIDS and, 74–75, 77–79; elements of, 10; foreign aid and, 90–97; IMF and, 11–12; migration and, 117–18, 126–31; poverty and, 11–15, 176–84; prioritarians and, 10–15; rent-seeking and, 14; World Bank and, 11–12
country policy and institutional assessment (CPIA) scores, 91–92

democracy, 23, 178
democratic peace theory, 99–100
difference principle, 37–38, 97–98
distributive justice, 3–6; intellectual property rights and, 71–79; trade and, 48–49

Doctors without Borders (Méde-cins sans Frontieres), 73
Doha Development Round, 74, 177
Dollar, David, 91–96
drugs. *See* pharmaceuticals
Dutch East Indies Company, 151
Dworkin, Richard, xvi
Dworkin, Ronald, 4

economic justice: balance-of-payments support and, 109–10; balance-of-power theory and, 27–28; central authority and, 4–5; communitarianism and, 6–10, 74–75; cosmopolitanism and, 10–15; developing countries and, 64–71; distributive justice and, 3–6, 48–49, 71–79; domestic, 23–26; as equality of opportunity, 39–44; foreign aid and, 86–113; free trade and, 49–57; game theory and, 49–57; GATT and, 58–60; international models for, 3–23; international theory for, 23–44; labor standards and, 134–45; multilateral arrangements and, 25; national welfare model and, 74–75; political change and, 190–95; poverty

reduction and, 176–84; reform and, 176–95; social safety nets and, 109–10; supranational authority and, 25–26; TRIPS and, 63–64; war and, 28
Economist, The, 114, 125–26
education, 9–10, 133, 142, 183
efficiency, 60–61
egalitarian concerns, 60–61
Egypt, 65
embedded liberalism, 24
environmental issues, 115–16; corporate social responsibility and, 164–68; Global Reporting Initiative and, 165–66; United Nations Global Compact and, 168–73
equality of opportunity, 90; economic justice and, 39–44; foreign aid and, 101–7; migration and, 115–34
"Ethical Globalization Initiative" (U.N. program), 1
ethics, 22–23, 47; central authority and, 4–5; common ground and, 1–2; communitarianism and, 6–10; concessions and, 61–63, 65; corporate social responsibility and, 164–68; cosmopolitanism and, 10–15; diplomacy and, 57–64;

ethics (*cont.*)
distributive principles and, 3–6; economic justice and, 3–23 (*see also* economic justice); equality of opportunity and, 39–44, 101–7; foreign direct investment (FDI) and, 147–74; migration and, 115–34; national welfare and, 80–83; need for, 1–2; poverty and, 176–84 (*see also* poverty); power issues and, 30–44; private standards and, 164–68; real-world negotiations and, 57–64; reciprocity and, 30–44; reform and, 176–95; trade concessions and, 61–63; United Nations Global Compact and, 168–72; violence and, 28, 32–33
Ethiopia, 94
ethnic groups, 4
Europe and the Trade Needs of the Less Developed Countries (U.N. report), 68–69
European Treaty, 133
European Union: domestic crises and, 109; ethical scandals and, 1; foreign direct investment (FDI) and, 150; GATT and, 58–59; generalized system of preferences (GSPs) and, 69; labor standards and, 142; protectionism and, 1; reform and, 192; trade concessions and, 62–63; trade inequality of, 84
Evolution of Cooperation, The (Axelrod), 30
exclusion, 117–18

factor price equalization (FPE), 53
fairness: distributive justice and, 3–6, 48–49, 71–79; equal-opportunity approach and, 39–44, 90, 101–7, 115–34; foreign direct investment and, 157–63; game theory and, 32–33, 49–57; GATT and, 58–60, 65–69; international justice and, 49–57; migration and, 115–34; multinational enterprises and, 157–63; real-world negotiations and, 57–64. *See also* economic justice
Federal Reserve Bank of Minneapolis, 161
Fehr, Ernst, 36
Feis, Herbert, 139–40
Finger, J. Michael, 61–63
Finnemore, Martha, 179
foreign aid: balance-of-payments support and, 109–12; corruption and, 88; cosmopolitanism

and, 90–97; country policy and institutional assessment (CPIA) scores and, 91–92; democratic peace theory and, 99–100; domestic crises and, 108–12; duty of assistance and, 86, 90; effectiveness and, 112–13; equal opportunity approach to, 101–7; human rights and, 98–99; hunger and, 90; institutional regimes and, 97–101; international justice and, 88–90; international stability and, 108–12; Llavador-Roemer model and, 103–4; Marshall Plan and, 88; millennium challenge accounts and, 90; Millennium Development Goals and, 87, 90–91; normative theory and, 87–89; poverty-efficient allocation and, 91; protectionism and, 96; Rawlsian analysis and, 86, 90, 92, 97–101; reform and, 176–90; targeting and, 95; tariff barriers and, 106–7; trickle-down theories and, 93; World Bank and, 89; World Trade Organization and, 106; World War II era and, 88–89
foreign direct investment (FDI): bargaining process and, 151–57; corporate social responsibility and, 164–68; corruption and, 151–52; fairness in, 157–63; firm bargaining and, 151–57; future discounts and, 150; host country advantages and, 153; Multilateral Agreement on Investment (MAI) and, 157–63; multinational enterprises (MNEs) and, 147–49; nesting and, 156; one-shot deals and, 151–57; policy agenda for, 189–90; poverty reduction and, 179–80; private standards and, 164–68; reciprocity and, 157–58; self-regulation and, 164–68; state antagonism and, 152–53; subsidies and, 160–61; TAPLINE and, 154–55; technology and, 152; UNCTAD and, 158–59; United Nations Global Compact and, 168–73; World Bank and, 149–50
France, 13, 116, 164
Franck, Thomas, 147–49, 174
free trade: developing countries and, 64–71; equal-opportunity approach and, 101–7; game theory and, 49–50; income distribution and, 46–47; international justice and, 49–57;

free trade (*cont.*)
national welfare and, 80–83;
normative theory and, 46; policy bias and, 45–46; real-
world negotiations and, 57–
64; special interests and, 58.
See also trade

Gachter, Simon, 36
game theory, 84–85, 116; bargaining process and, 156–57;
diplomacy and, 57–64; factor
price equalization and, 53; fair
regimes and, 32–33; international justice and, 49–57; international relations theory
and, 30–37; labor standards
and, 139–40; migration and,
130; multinational enterprises
(MNEs) and, 157–58; opti-
mum tariff and, 52; potential
settlement region and, 52;
Rawlsian bargaining and, 49–
51, 53; reciprocity and, 30–
37, 157–58; social compact
and, 114–15
Gates, Bill, 12, 175
General Agreement on Tariffs
and Trade (GATT), 58–60,
65–69
generalized system of preferences (GSPs), 48, 69

genetically modified organisms,
115
Germany, 152, 204n85
Ghana, 59
Ghei, Nita, 33
Gladden, Washington, xi
globalization, 15–16: balance-of-
power theory and, 27–28;
communitarianism and, 6–10;
convergence and, 21; developing countries and, 64–71;
distributive justice and, 3–6;
domestic crises and, 108–12;
ethics and, 1–2 (*see also* ethics); foreign aid and, 86–113;
foreign direct investment
(FDI) and, 147–74; growth
and, 20–21; international economic justice and, 23–44; international regimes and, 184–
90; multinational enterprises
and, 147–49; reciprocity and,
30–44, 157–58; reform and,
176–95; social compacts in,
114–15; supranational authority and, 25–26; United Nations Global Compact and,
168–73; World War II era
and, 8
Globalization with a Human Face
(U.N. report), 2
Global Reporting Initiative,
165–66

"Global Resource Tax" (Pogge proposal), 12
governments. *See* states
Graham, Edward, 158–61
Great Depression, 110
Greenspan, Alan, 45
Group of 77, 69
growth, 19; classic models of, 66–67; communitarianism and, 8–10; equal-opportunity approach and, 101–7; foreign aid and, 86–113; free trade and, 20–21, 45; investment-led, 122; migration and, 122; poverty reduction and, 177; reform and, 176; technological inequalities and, 53–57
Guidelines for Multinational Enterprises, 157

Haberler, Gottfried, 67
Harrison, Glenn W., 80
Harvard Business School, 165
health insurance, 76–77
health issues, 116; AIDS and, 48, 71–79; distributive justice and, 48–49, 71–79; migration and, 133; pharmaceuticals and, 71–79; poverty and, 90
Hicks, John, 46–47
Hirshleifer, Jack, 28
Hobbes, Thomas, 5
Hoffmann, Stanley, 5–6

Hopkins, Raymond, 32–33
Howe, Roger, 49
Hudec, Robert, 70
human capital, 98–99, 147; civil liberties and, 21; corporate social responsibility and, 164–68; labor standards and, 134–45 (*see also* labor); migration and, 115–34; poverty and, 175–84 (*see also* poverty); property rights and, 21; United Nations Global Compact and, 168–73
Human Rights Watch, 147
Hume, David, 203n78
hunger, 111, 179
Huntington, Samuel, 190–91
Hurrell, Andrew, 34

illiteracy, 90
income distribution, 16, 20; democracies and, 23; economic justice and, 3–6 (*see also* economic justice); equality of opportunity and, 39–44; foreign aid and, 86–113; free trade and, 46–47; lump-sum transfers and, 81–82; policy agenda for, 175–95; poverty reduction and, 176–84; remittances and, 123, 131–32; TAPLINE and, 154–55; technological inequalities and, 53–57

India, 72, 93–94, 165
infant industries, 67
intellectual property rights, 55; distributive justice and, 71–79; pharmaceutical products and, 48, 71–79; TRIPS and, 63–64, 71–73
International Chamber of Commerce, 165
"International Financial Facility" (Brown proposal), 13
international justice: equal-opportunity approach and, 101–7; foreign aid and, 88–90; free trade and, 49–57; game theory and, 49–57; labor standards and, 139–45; migration and, 115–34; potential settlement region and, 52; reform and, 184–90; stability and, 108–12. See also economic justice
International Labor Organization (ILO), 25, 86, 141–42, 189
International Monetary Fund (IMF), 11–12, 18; domestic crises and, 109–12; poverty reduction and, 177, 180; reform and, 187–88
International Organization for Migration (IOM), 132

international relations theory: anarchy and, 30; cooperation theories and, 28–44; difference principle and, 37–38; economic justice and, 23–44; equality of opportunity and, 39–44; free trade and, 46; game theory and, 30–37; reciprocity and, 30–44; self interest and, 28; war and, 28
investment: BITs and, 159; distributive justice and, 5–6; Multilateral Agreement on Investment (MAI) and, 157–63; multinational enterprises (MNEs) and, 147–49; nesting and, 156; normative theory and, 147; state reneging and, 149. See also foreign direct investment (FDI)
Iraq, 154–55
Iraq Petroleum Company, 154
Irwin, Douglas, 81
Israel, 128

Japan, 60–61, 63, 69, 98
Johnson, Harry, 64–65
justice: distributive, 5–6, 48–49, 71–79; economic, 20–23 (see also economic justice); equality of opportunity and, 39–44, 90, 101–7, 115–34; foreign aid and, 86–113; game theory

and, 49–57; international, 108–12 (*see also* international justice); labor and, 134–39; migration and, 117–25; reform and, 184–90

Kanbur, Ravi, 80
Kell, Georg, 169
Keohane, Robert, 30–33, 37
Keynes, John Maynard, 134–35
Kindleberger, Charles, 152–55
Kissinger, Henry, 34
Koremenos, Barbara, 35
Krugman, Paul, 55–56

labor, xi, 84–85, 146; brain drain and, 118; child, 24, 142–43; China and, 20; communitarianism and, 7–8; corporate social responsibility and, 164–68; cosmopolitanism and, 10–11; economic justice and, 134–39; escape clauses and, 7–8; International Labor Organization and, 25, 86, 141–42, 189; level playing field for, 2; migration and, 115–34; minimum wage and, 114; multinational enterprises (MNEs) and, 140–41, 152; normative theory and, 115–16; openness effects and, 9–10; quotas and, 179; reform and, 188–89; re-

mittances and, 123, 131–32; SA8000 code and, 165; skilled, 121–23, 127, 142; social compact and, 143–45; standards for, 25, 134–45, 189; technology and, 123, 136; unemployment and, 49, 123, 146; United Nations Global Compact and, 168–73; wage flexibility and, 136
Lalman, David, 27
Law of Peoples, The (Rawls), 19–20, 97, 119–20, 182
lawyers, 106
Lebanon, 154–55
less developed countries (LDCs): AIDS and, 71–79; communitarianism and, 74–76; foreign direct investment (FDI) and, 147–74; generalized system of preferences (GSPs) and, 69–70; Group of 77 and, 69; international trade and, 64–71; MAI packages and, 157–63; reform and, 184–90; regime structure and, 65–66; United Nations and, 66–69
level playing field, xi–xii, xv, 22–23; consensus for, 2; differing views on, 2–3; labor standards and, 25, 134–45, 189;

level playing field (*cont.*)
migration and, 115–34; policy
agenda for, 175–95; poverty
reduction and, 11–12, 176–84.
See also ethics
Lewis, David, 38
Lewis, John P., 66
liberal internationalism, xii–xiii,
74–75; AIDS policies and, 78–
79; balance-of-power theory
and, 27–28; basic elements of,
15–23; communitarianism
and, 6–10; concessions and,
61–62; cosmopolitanism and,
10–15; developing countries
and, 64–71; economic justice
models and, 3–23; equality of
opportunity and, 39–44, 101–
7; foreign aid and, 97–107;
free trade and, 20–21; game
theory and, 30–37 (see also
game theory); GATT and,
58–60; generalized system of
preferences (GSPs) and, 69–
70; labor standards and, 137–
38; migration and, 131–34; national welfare and, 80–83; Pareto optimality and, 81; poverty reduction and, 183–84;
real-world negotiations and,
59–64; reciprocity and, xiv–xv,
30–44; sovereignty and, 16–

17; statist approach and, 15–
16; supranational authority
and, 25–26; war and, 28
Lipson, Charles, 35
Llavador, Humberto, 41–42, 90,
103–4
Lumsdaine, David, 88–89

macroeconomic stabilization,
103
Markusen, James, 157
Marshall Plan, 88
Medicines Act, 71–72
Meier, Gerald, 67
mercantilism, 47, 61–62
Mexico, 133
migration, 115–16, 146; absorptive capacity and, 126; brain
drain and, 118; communitarianism and, 118, 125; cosmopolitanism and, 117–18, 126–
31; economic effects of, 124;
economic welfare approach
to, 120–25, 128–31; education
and, 133; family reunification
and, 125; human rights and,
117–18, 123–24, 128–33; International Organization for
Migration and, 132; justice in,
117–25; liberal internationalism and, 131–34; limitations
on, 125–26; motivations for,
117–21; national welfare and,

125–28; normative theory and, 115–16; population pressures and, 123, 126; prioritarian model and, 131–34; Rawlsian analysis and, 119–20; reform and, 188; remittances and, 123, 131–32; skilled labor and, 121–23, 127; social services and, 133; taxes and, 132; unemployment and, 123

Milanovic, Branko, 10

Mill, John Stuart, 23, 81

Millennium Development Goals (MDGs), 2, 87, 90–91, 113, 177, 180–81

Miller, David, 102

monopolies, 54

morality. *See* ethics

most favored nation (MFN) status, 58, 69

Multilateral Agreement on Investment (MAI), 157–63, 173

multinational enterprises (MNEs), 147–48; bargaining process and, 151–57; corporate social responsibility and, 164–68; fairness and, 157–63; firm bargaining and, 151–57; game theory and, 157–58; Global Reporting Initiative and, 165–66; governing of, 157–63; host country advantages and, 153; MAI packages and, 157–63; OECD and, 156–57; private standards and, 164–68; reciprocity and, 157–58; self-regulation and, 164–68; UNCTAD and, 158–59; United Nations Global Compact and, 168–73

Myrdal, Gunnar, 89, 175

National Health Service, 75

national security, 178, 180

natural resources, xii; distributive justice and, 5–6; Rawls on, 19–20; war and, 28

Nike, 142

nongovernmental organizations (NGOs), 72–73; Amnesty International and, 147; Apparel Industry Partnership and, 165; corporate social responsibility and, 164–68; Global Reporting Initiative and, 165–66; Human Rights Watch and, 147; multinational enterprises and, 147–48; Oxfam and, 12, 45, 73, 162–63; poverty reduction and, 179–80, 184; reform and, 194–95; Responsible Care and, 165; Save the Children and, 12; United

NGOs (*cont.*)
   Nations Global Compact and, 168–73
normative theory, 46; democratic peace theory and, 99–100; foreign aid and, 87–89; global revolution and, 175; international regimes and, 184–90; investment and, 147; migration and, 115–16
norm entrepreneurs, 179–80
Nowak, Martin A., 35–36
Nozick, Robert, 4–5
nuclear power, 116

obesity, 116
one-shot deals, 151–57
Organization for Economic Cooperation and Development (OECD), 156–60, 173
O'Rourke, Kevin, 129
Oxfam, 12, 45, 73, 162–63

Page, Karen, 35–36
Pareto, Vilifredo, 81
Parfit, Derek, 3, 10
Parisi, Francesco, 33
peace zones, 28
Penrose, Edith, 153–54
Pharmaceutical Manufacturers Association of South Africa, 72
pharmaceuticals: activists and, 48; AIDS and, 48, 71–79; corporate responsibility and, 164–65; generics and, 72; intellectual property rights and, 48–49, 71–79
Pogge, Thomas, 10–12, 26
policies: anarchy and, 30; balance-of-payments support and, 109–12; balance-of-power theory and, 27–28; bias and, 45–46; Bretton Woods, 7, 66; communitarianism and, 6–10; cooperation theories and, 28–44; corporate social responsibility and, 164–68; cosmopolitanism and, 3, 10–15; country policy and institutional assessment (CPIA) scores and, 91–92; developing countries and, 64–71; diplomacy and, 57–64; discrimination and, 64–65; distributive justice and, 3–6, 48–49, 71–79; domestic crises and, 108–12; equal-opportunity approach and, 101–7; equity and, 60–61; as ethical scandal, 1; European Treaty and, 133; foreign aid and, 86–113; foreign direct investment (FDI) and, 147–74; GATT and, 58–60, 65–69; generalized system of preferences and, 48; Guide-

lines for Multinational Enterprises and, 157; international justice and, 23–44, 49–57; labor standards and, 134–45; Marshall Plan and, 88; mercantilism and, 47, 61–62; migration, 115–34; millennium challenge accounts and, 90; Multilateral Agreement on Investment (MAI) and, 157–63; national welfare and, 80; openness and, 9–10, 49, 59, 80; potential settlement region and, 52; poverty effects and, 45–46, 176–84; protectionism and, 86; real-world negotiations and, 57–64; reciprocity and, 30–44; reform and, 176–95; share-the-wealth schemes and, 66; status quo and, 27–28; technological inequalities and, 53–57; trade expectations and, 29–30; trickle-down theories and, 93; United Nations Global Compact and, 168–73; war and, 28

politics, xiv; activists and, 1, 12, 48 (*see also* activism); balance-of-power theory and, 27–28; bargaining and, 151–57; cooperation theories and, 28–44; corporate social responsibility and, 164–68; cosmopolitanism and, 10–15; democracies and, 178; democratic peace theory and, 99–100; diplomacy and, 57–64; distributive justice and, 3–6, 48–49, 71–79; domestic crises and, 108–12; egalitarian concerns and, 60–61; game theory and, 30–37, 49–57; human rights and, 98–99; international justice and, 26–44, 49–57; international regimes and, 184–90; labor standards and, 134–45; lobbyists and, 179; migration and, 115–34; military retaliation and, 51–52; national security and, 178, 180; poverty reduction and, 176–84; Rawlsian bargaining and, 49–51; reciprocity and, 30–44; reform and, 176–95; reneged agreements and, 149; special interest groups and, 116, 178–79; United Nations and, 66–67; violence and, 28, 32–33

potential settlement region (PSR), 28, 52

poverty, xiii, 175; AIDS and, 71–79; communitarianism and, 7; cosmopolitanism and, 11–15, 90–97; disease and, 90;

poverty (*cont.*)
  distributive justice and, 48–49, 71–79; equality of opportunity and, 39–44, 101–7; extent of, 176; foreign aid and, 86–113; foreign direct investment and, 148; hunger and, 90; illiteracy and, 90; Millennium Development Goals and, 177, 180–81; Multilateral Agreement on Investment (MAI) and, 157–63; national welfare and, 80; Oxfam and, 162–63; policy bias and, 45–46; reduction policies for, 90–97, 176–84; special interest groups and, 178–79; trickle-down theories and, 93; "veil of ignorance" and, 19; World War II era and, 88–89
Poverty Reduction Growth Facility (PRGF), 181–82
Prebisch, Raul, 66–67
prioritarian model, 3, 74–75; cosmopolitanism and, 10–15; foreign aid and, 91; migration and, 125, 131–34
protectionism, xi, 86, 189; agriculture and, 1; foreign aid and, 96; poverty reduction and, 183–84
Public Choice school, 166–67

Puchala, Donald, 32–33
Putnam, Robert, 57

quotas, 179

Rawls, John, 49–51, 53; burdened societies and, 97; democratic peace theory and, 99–100; difference principle of, 97–98; duty of assistance and, 86, 90, 182–83; economic justice and, 19–20, 24, 37; foreign aid and, 86, 90, 92, 97–101; human rights and, 98–99; migration and, 119–20; poverty reduction and, 182–83
realist theory, 38
reciprocity, xiv–xv, 83; concessions and, 61–63, 65; diffuse, 31, 37–38, 48; egalitarian concerns and, 60–61; equality of opportunity and, 39–44; game theory and, 30–37, 157–58; generalized system of preferences (GSPs) and, 69–70; international relations theory and, 30–44; multinational enterprises (MNEs) and, 157–58; overall, 61; qua equivalence and, 65; reform and, 187; specific, 30–34, 61; world trade order and, 58–60

Reebok, 142

reform: international regimes and, 184–90; nongovernmental organizations (NGOs) and, 194–95; policy agenda for, 176–95; political change and, 190–95; poverty reduction and, 176–84; rarity of, 190–91

religion, 4, 13, 177, 179

remittances, 123, 131–32

rent-seeking, 14, 166–67

Responsible Care, 165

Robinson, Mary, 1

Rodrik, Dani, 8, 18, 46, 108, 129, 136

Roemer, John, 49; economic justice and, 40–42; foreign aid and, 90, 103–4; labor and, 117–19

Ruggie, John Gerard, 7, 24, 164, 168–69, 171

Russia, 92, 96, 135

Rutherford, Thomas F., 80

SA8000 code, 165

Sahlins, Marshall, 32

Samuelson, Paul, 57

Saudi Arabia, 26, 154–55

Save the Children, 12

savings, 122

Schelling, Thomas, 4, 35

security, 138–39, 178, 180

self-regulation, 164–68

Sen, Amartya, 98

share-the-wealth schemes, 66

Sigmund, Karl, 35–36

Sikkink, Kathryn, 179

Singapore, 100–101

smoking, 116

Snidal, Douglas, 35

social liberals: liberal internationalism and, 15–23; statist approach and, 15–16

social responsibility, 164–67; poverty reduction and, 176–84; reform and, 176–95; United Nations Global Compact and, 168–73

social safety nets, 109–10

Soligo, Ronald, 120

Solimano, Andres, 122

South Africa, 71–75

Soviet Union, 92, 96, 135

Spar, Debora, 147, 165–66

special differential status (S&D), 48, 70–71

special interest groups, 58, 116, 178–79

Standard Oil Trust, 151

states: anarchy and, 30; autonomous societies and, 116; balance-of-payments support and, 109–12; balance-of-power theory and, 27–28;

states (*cont.*)

BITs and, 159; central authority and, 4–5; cooperation theories and, 28–44; corporate social responsibility and, 164–68; cosmopolitanism and, 10–15; democracies and, 23; destiny control by, 21–22; domestic crises and, 108–12; economic justice and, 3–23 (*see also* economic justice); equality of opportunity and, 39–44,101–7; firm bargaining and, 151–57; foreign aid and, 86–113; foreign direct investment (FDI) and, 147–74; game theory and, 30–37 (*see also* game theory); international stability and, 108–12; labor and, 134–45; liberal internationalism and, 15–16 (*see also* liberal internationalism); migration and, 115–34; Multilateral Agreement on Investment (MAI) and, 157–63; multinational enterprises (MNEs) and, 147–49, 157–63; public good and, 144–45; reciprocity and, 30–44; reneged agreements by, 149; respect for sovereignty and, 16–17;

self interest and, 28; social compact and, 114–15, 135, 143–45; social services and, 133; society of, 16–17; sovereignty and, 16–17; stochastic uncertainty and, 30, 33–34,36–37; subsidies and, 160–61; supranational authority and, 25–26; United Nations Global Compact and, 168–73; war and, 28. *See also* politics

statist approach, 15–16

Stiglitz, Joseph, 1

subsidies, 160–61

Summers, Lawrence, 21–22

supranational authority, 25–26

survival rights, 138–39

Sweden, 20–21, 92

Syria, 155

tariffs, 106–7; agriculture and, 67–68; escalation of, 67–68; GATT and, 58–60, 65–69; optimum tariff and, 52; TAPLINE and, 154–55; trade concessions and, 63

Tarr, David G., 80

taxes, 75, 132, 183

technology, 20–21; distributive inequalities and, 53–57; foreigndirect investment (FDI) and, 152; labor and, 123, 136;

medical, 76–77; modern communications and, 179–80; nuclear power and, 116
terrorism, 180
textile quotas, 179
Thatcher, Margaret, 75
tit-for-tat strategy, 30
"Tobin Tax" (Chirac proposal), 13
Tokyo Round (trade negotiations), 60–61, 63, 69
trade: communitarianism and, 6–10; concessions and, 61–63, 65, 83, 187; cooperation theories and, 28–29; developing countries and, 64–71; economic justice and, 3–23; efficiency concerns and, 45, 60–61; egalitarian concerns and, 60–61; equality of opportunity and, 39–44; equity and, 60–61; factor price equalization and, 53; foreign direct investment (FDI) and, 147–74; GATT and, 58–60, 65–69; growth and, 20–21 (see also growth); intellectual property rights and, 55, 71–79; international justice and, 49–57; international regimes and, 184–90; labor and, 114, 141 (see also labor); liberal internationalism and, 20–21 (see also liberal internationalism); national welfare and, 80–83; openness and, 59, 80, 103; optimum tariff and, 52; peace zones and, 28; policy effects and, 29–30; poverty effects and, 45–46; real-world negotiations and, 57–64; reciprocity and, 30–44, 58–60; regime structure and, 48, 65–84; special and differential status (S&D) and, 48; technological inequalities and, 53–57; World Trade Organization and, 58–59
trade-related intellectual property rights (TRIPS), 63–64, 71–73
Trans-Arabian Pipeline (TAPLINE), 154–55
trickle-down theories, 93

Uganda, 94
ultimatum game, 35–36
United Kingdom, 12–13, 121, 124
United Nations, 173; Commission on Europe, 68–69; Conference on Trade and Development (UNCTAD) and, 69,

United Nations (*cont.*)
158–59; Development Decade and, 69; domestic crises and, 109; Global Compact and, 156–57, 168–73; High Commissioner for Human Rights, 1; less developed countries and, 66–67; Millennium Development Goals and, 2, 87, 90–91, 113, 177, 180–81
United States, 2, 29, 75; AIDS and, 75–76; communitarianism and, 7–8; corporate social responsibility and, 164; ethical scandals and, 1; foreign direct investment (FDI) and, 150; GATT and, 58–59; generalized system of preferences (GSPs) and, 69–70; George W. Bush administration and, 90; investment policies and, 161; labor standards and, 142; migration and, 121, 124–25, 133; millennium challenge accounts and, 90; obesity in, 116; optimum tariff and, 52; reform and, 192; state investment competition in, 161–62; trade adjustment assistance and, 7–8; trade concessions and, 62–63; trade inequality of, 84

Uruguay Round (trade negotiations), 61–63
utilitarianism, xiii, 81

Varian, Hal, 4
Vernon, Raymond, 155, 161–62
Versailles Treaty, 204n85
violence, 28, 32–33, 44, 51–52, 204n85
voting, 47, 114, 125

Walzer, Michael, 127
war, 28
Weiner, Myron, 118, 126–27
welfare, xii–xiii; AIDS and, 71–79; democracies and, 23; effects on national, 3; equal-opportunity approach and, 101–7; foreign aid and, 86–113; international economic justice and, 23–44; international trade and, 80–83; maximizing policies for, 47; migration and, 115–34; reform and, 176–90; state negotiations and, 17–18 (*see also* states)
Wilcox, Clair, 65–66
Williamson, Jeffrey, 129
Wolfensohn, James, 1, 176
World Bank, 1, 10, 61–62, 122; Bretton Woods and, 66; cosmopolitanism and, 11–12; country policy and institu-

tional assessment (CPIA) scores and, 91–92; domestic crises and, 109–10; foreign aid and, 89; foreign direct investment (FDI) and, 149–50; poverty reduction and, 176–81; reform and, 176, 187–88

World Economic Forum, 169

World Trade Organization (WTO), xiii–xiv, 18, 58–59, 64; cooperation theories and, 30–31; foreign aid and, 106; poverty reduction and, 177; reform and, 176, 192; TRIPS and, 72

World War II era, 8, 18; domestic crises and, 110; foreign aid and, 88–89; less developed countries and, 65; Marshall Plan and, 88; optimum tariff and, 52; regime design and, 65–66

Yoffie, David, 147, 165–66